The Severans analyses the colourful
decline of the Roman empire during the
reign of the Severans, the first non-Italian
dynasty. In his learned and exciting style,
Michael Grant describes the foreign wars
waged against the Alemanni and the
Persians, and the remarkable personalities
of the imperial family. Thus the reader can
encounter Julia Domna's alleged literary
circle, or Elagabalus' curious private life –
which included dancing in the streets,
marrying a vestal virgin and smothering
his enemies with rose petals.

With its carefully selected illustrations,
maps and extensive further reading list,
this book will appeal to the student of
ancient history as well as to the
interested general reader.

THE SEVERANS

THE SEVERANS

The changed Roman empire

Michael Grant

London and New York

First published 1996
by Routledge
11 New Fetter Lane, London EC4P 4EE

Simultaneously published in the USA and Canada
by Routledge
29 West 35th Street, New York, NY 10001
Routledge is an International Thomson Publishing company

Phototypeset in Garamond by Intype London Ltd
Printed and bound in Great Britain by
Biddles Ltd, Guildford and King's Lynn

British Library Cataloguing in Publication Data
A catalogue record for this book is available from the British Library

Library of Congress Cataloguing in Publication Data
Grant, Michael.
The Severans: the changed Roman empire/Michael Grant.
p.   cm.
Includes bibliographical references and index.
1. Rome–History–Severans, 193–235.   I. Title.
DG298.G73   1996
937'.07—dc20   95–45816
ISBN 0–415–12772–6

CONTENTS

List of plates		vii
List of maps		ix
INTRODUCTION		1
1	SEPTIMIUS SEVERUS AND THE STRUGGLE FOR POWER	7
2	THE PRAETORIANS AND THEIR PREFECTS: PLAUTIANUS	14
3	THE GESTURES OF SEPTIMIUS	18
4	THE SUCCESSORS	21
5	THE PROVINCES AND ITALY: THE *CONSTITUTIO ANTONINIANA*	28
6	THE ARMY: THE MILITARY MONARCHY	34
7	FINANCE	39
8	THE SYRIAN WOMEN	45
9	THE LAWYERS	49
10	THE NOVEL: LONGUS	53
11	ART AND ARCHITECTURE	60
12	PAGANISM AND CHRISTIANITY	74
	Epilogue	85
	Appendix: the literary sources	87
	List of emperors	91
	List of abbreviations	92

CONTENTS

Notes   93
Further reading   107
Index   111

PLATES

1 Pertinax. *Dupondius*
2 Didius Julianus. *Sestertius*
3 Septimius Severus. Bust
4 Septimius Severus. *Sestertius*
5 Julia Domna. Bust
6 Septimius Severus and Julia Domna. *Aureus*
7 Septimius Severus, Julia Domna, Caracalla and Geta. *Aureus*
8 Geta (?). Bust
9 Geta. *Sestertius*
10 Pescennius Niger. *Denarius*
11 Clodius Albinus. *Aureus*
12 Caracalla. Bust
13 Alexander III the Great. Gold medallion
14 Macrinus. Bust
15 Diadumenian. Coin
16 Elagabalus. Bust
17 Elagabalus. *Aureus*
18 Elagabalus. *Aureus*
19 Julia Paula. *Denarius*
20 Aquilia Severa. *Sestertius*
21 Julia Maesa. *Denarius*
22 Severus Alexander. Bust
23 Severus Alexander. Statue
24 Severus Alexander. *Dupondius*
25 Julia Mamaea. Bust
26 Julia Mamaea. Base silver (billon) medallion
27 The Arch of Septimius Severus in the Forum
28 The Arch of Septimius Severus at Lepcis Magna: relief of the
   emperor in his chariot

29 The Sanctuary of Jupiter Heliopolitanus, Heliopolis (Baalbek)
30 The theatre at Sabratha
31 The Baths of Caracalla, Rome
32 The Arch of Caracalla, Cuicul (Djemila), north Africa

MAPS

1 The Roman empire under the Severans   x
2 Italy   xi
3 The western provinces   xii
4 North Africa   xiii
5 Eastern Europe   xiv
6 Asia Minor   xv
7 The east   xvi

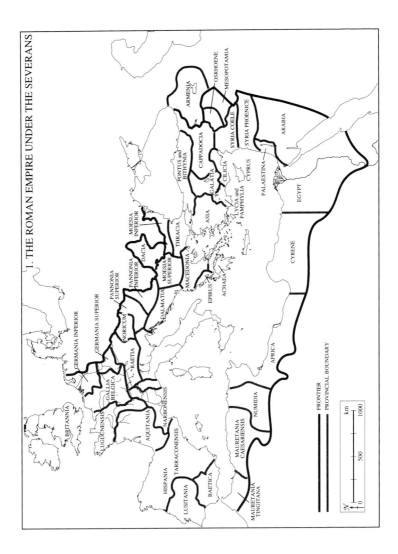

1. THE ROMAN EMPIRE UNDER THE SEVERANS

BRITANNIA
GERMANIA INFERIOR
GERMANIA SUPERIOR
GALLIA BELGICA
LUGDUNENSIS
NORICUM
RAETIA
AQUITANIA
NARBONENSIS
PANNONIA SUPERIOR
PANNONIA INFERIOR
DALMATIA
DACIA
MOESIA INFERIOR
MOESIA SUPERIOR
THRACIA
MACEDONIA
EPIRUS
ACHAEA
HISPANIA TARRACONENSIS
LUSITANIA
BAETICA
MAURETANIA TINGITANA
MAURETANIA CAESARIENSIS
NUMIDIA
AFRICA
CYRENE
EGYPT
ARMENIA
OSRHOENE
MESOPOTAMIA
CAPPADOCIA
PONTUS and BITHYNIA
GALATIA
CILICIA
ASIA
LYCIA and PAMPHYLIA
SYRIA COELE
SYRIA PHOENICE
CYPRUS
PALAESTINA
ARABIA

FRONTIER
PROVINCIAL BOUNDARY

km
0 500 1000

x

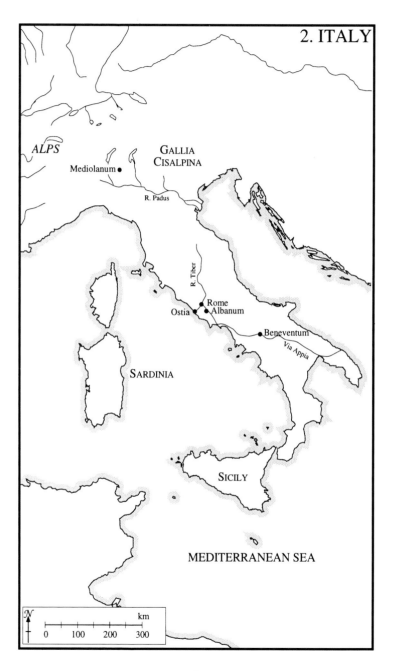

2. ITALY

ALPS

GALLIA CISALPINA

Mediolanum ●

R. Padus

R. Tiber

Rome
Ostia ● ● Albanum

● Beneventum

Via Appia

SARDINIA

SICILY

MEDITERRANEAN SEA

N

km

0   100   200   300

3. THE WESTERN PROVINCES

CALEDONIA
R. Tava
Carpow
R. Bodotria
Hadrian's Wall
Castlesteads
Eburacum
Deva
BRITANNIA
Isca Silurum
GERMANIA
R. Rhenus
GERMANIA INFERIOR
GALLIA BELGICA
ALAMANNI
Moguntiacum
LUGDUNENSIS
GERMANIA SUPERIOR
Tinurtium
BAY OF BISCAY
Lugdunum
R. Rhodanus
HISPANIA TARRACONENSIS
LUSITANIA
BAETICA

N
km
0 100 200 300 400 500

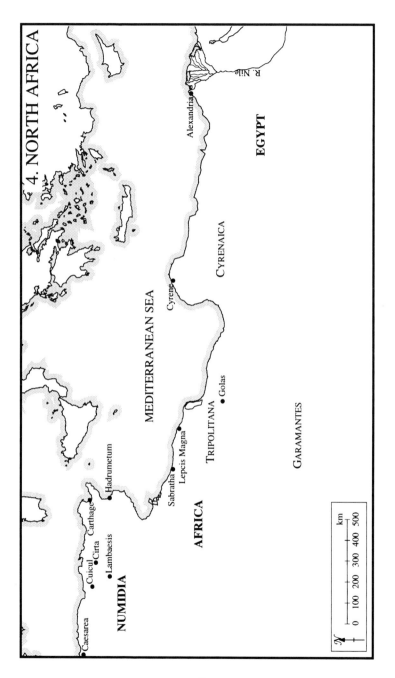

4. NORTH AFRICA

NUMIDIA

Caesarea

Cuicul
Cirta
Lambaesis

Carthage

Hadrumetum

AFRICA

Sabratha
Lepcis Magna

TRIPOLITANA

Golas

GARAMANTES

MEDITERRANEAN SEA

Cyrene

CYRENAICA

Alexandria

EGYPT

R. Nile

km

0 100 200 300 400 500

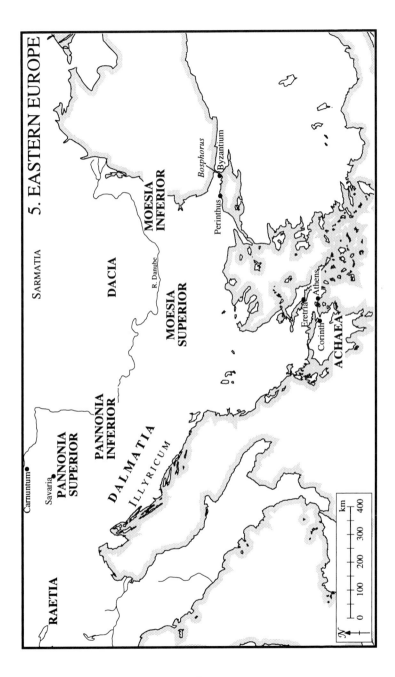

5. EASTERN EUROPE

RAETIA

PANNONIA
SUPERIOR

Carnuntum

Savaria

PANNONIA
INFERIOR

DALMATIA

ILLYRICUM

SARMATIA

DACIA

R. Danube

MOESIA
SUPERIOR

MOESIA
INFERIOR

Bosphorus
Byzantium

Perinthus

Eretria

Athens

Corinth

ACHAEA

km
0   100   200   300   400

N

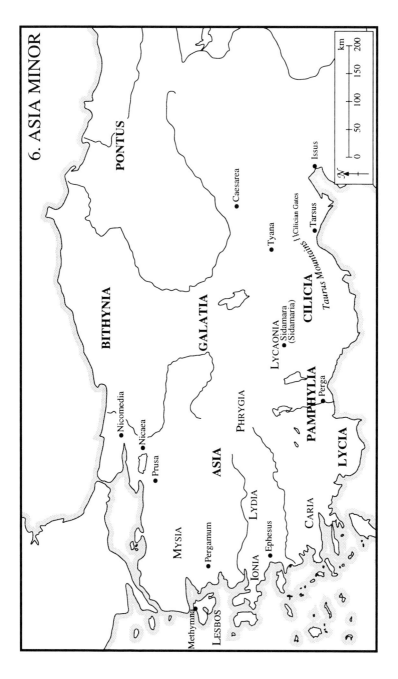

6. ASIA MINOR

PONTUS

BITHYNIA

GALATIA

Caesarea

Tyana

Nicomedia
Nicaea
Prusa

PHRYGIA

LYCAONIA
Sidamara
(Sidamaria)

CILICIA

Taurus Mountains

Clilician Gates

Tarsus

Issus

ASIA

MYSIA
Pergamum

LYDIA

IONIA
Ephesus

CARIA

PAMPHYLIA
Perga

LYCIA

Methymna
LESBOS

km
0 50 100 150 200

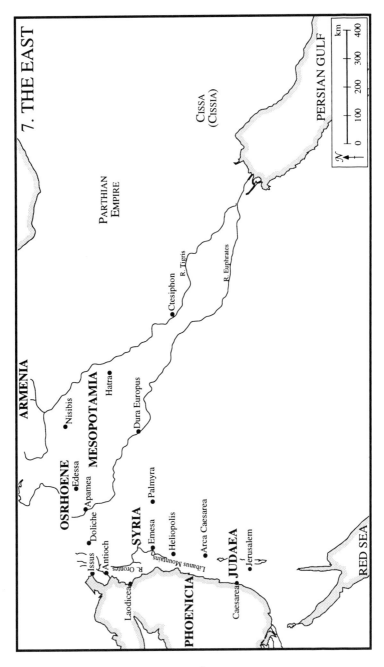

7. THE EAST

PERSIAN GULF

PARTHIAN EMPIRE

CISSA (CISSIA)

ARMENIA

MESOPOTAMIA

OSRHOENE

SYRIA

PHOENICIA

JUDAEA

RED SEA

•Nisibis

•Edessa

•Apamea

Doliche

Hatra•

•Dura Europus

Ctesiphon•

R. Tigris

R. Euphrates

Issus•
Antioch•
•Emesa
•Palmyra
•Heliopolis
•Arca Caesarea
•Jerusalem

Laodicea•

R. Orontes

Libanus Mountains

Caesarea•

km
0 100 200 300 400

xvi

INTRODUCTION

The end of the Antonine period in AD 192[1] marked what could be
called the termination of the high-water mark of the Roman empire.
It has always seemed strange to many that Marcus Aurelius (161–80),
a clever man, should have been so besotted by the dynastic, paternal
principle that he left the empire to his inadequate son Commodus
(180–92). But the murder of Commodus not only marked the
conclusion of the Antonine house, properly so-called, but ushered
in a period of civil war and imperial chaos, marked by a number of
short-lived reigns and attempted reigns.

The first of these régimes was that of Commodus's immediate
successor Pertinax, emperor from January to March 193 (Plate 1).
His father was a freed slave, Helvius Successus, who allegedly named
his son 'Pertinax' to celebrate his own perseverance in the timber
trade. After a spell as a school-teacher, the future emperor Pertinax
joined the army, rising to the command of units in Syria, Britain and
Moesia. Then, following civilian posts (procuratorships of knightly
(equestrian) rank in Italy and Dacia), he commanded legionary
groups in Pannonia, where he fought against the Germans, subsequently becoming a legionary commander in Raetia, consul in
174 or 175, and then governor of Upper and Lower Moesia
(combined) and Dacia and Syria, and subsequently commander of
(mutinous) troops in Britain, proconsul of Africa and city prefect
of Rome. In 192 he became consul for a second time.

It is doubted whether Pertinax was unaware of the plot to murder
Commodus on the last night of that year. In any case the praetorian
prefect (on these see Chapter 2) invited Pertinax to accept the throne,
whereupon he hastened to the praetorian camp, and promised the
guardsmen a substantial donative, so that they duly acclaimed him
as emperor. Then he visited the senate, which was obliged to concur.

But Pertinax soon became unpopular owing to a policy of financial entrenchment, necessitated by Commodus's extravagance. In particular, he lost the support of the praetorian guard, since he had failed to pay them more than 50 per cent of the donatives he had promised them. So they murdered him, apparently on 28 March 193.

His successor was Didius Julianus, who reigned from late March until June 193 (Plate 2). Marcus Didius Severus Julianus was the son of a man who belonged to one of the leading families of Mediolanum (Milan). His mother was a north African. Before becoming emperor, Didius Julianus had a lengthy and prominent public career. He commanded a legion at Moguntiacum (Mainz), was governor of Gallia Belgica in about 170, and became consul, with Pertinax, in 174 or 175. Then he was appointed, one after another, to the governorships of Dalmatia, Lower Germany, Bithynia-Pontus and Africa (189–90), where he succeeded Pertinax.

After the latter's accession to the throne, followed soon afterwards by his death, Didius Julianus made his own bid for the empire, which has gone down in history as a disgraceful episode. In successful competition with Titus Flavius Sulpicianus, the father-in-law of the late Pertinax and prefect of the city, Didius Julianus bought the job of emperor by offering the praetorian guard 25,000 *sestertii* (10,000 *denarii*) a head, which he gave them along with another 5,000 *sestertii*. Yet this must be seen in perspective. Even the high-minded Marcus Aurelius and his colleague Lucius Verus had given the guardsmen 20,000 *sestertii* each when they came to the throne (161), and since then there had been a good deal of inflation (Chapter 7).

However, this elevation of Didius Julianus to the purple aroused discontent among the inhabitants of the capital, despite promises that they, too, would receive considerable sums of money. And their discontent must have spurred on the rival ambitions of Septimius Severus and Pescennius Niger, governors of Upper Pannonia and Syria respectively, each of whom declared himself emperor in Didius Julianus's place.

The most immediate danger came from Septimius, whom Didius first declared a public enemy, thereafter, however, sending envoys to speak with him, and, finally, offering him joint tenure of the throne, which Septimius rejected. Didius then approached the praetorian guardsmen (promising them immunity for the murder of Pertinax if they handed over his actual assassins). However, he was deposed by the senate, which sent a soldier into the palace to assassinate him.

In my book on the *Antonines* their epoch was described as a time of transition. By the time of Septimius Severus (AD 193–211) the empire had completely changed. He and his successors (Chapter 4) belonged to an epoch when life was tougher and the whole Roman world was at stake. After the Severans, it seemed to collapse. But this collapse was only temporary, to a large extent because of the massive work which Septimius had done to shore the empire up, especially after he had got rid of his too powerful praetorian prefect, Plautianus (Chapter 2). So we have here a period in which one of the most able of all the rulers, Septimius, put himself in charge. He was followed, however, by four inadequate men who frittered all his achievements away.

Not that Septimius, by any means, was perfect. He accomplished one feat of mighty disinformation, or in other words created an enormous lie, by declaring that he was the son of Marcus Aurelius, which he was not (Chapter 3). But this he did quite deliberately, in order to bolster up his position and that of his dynasty.

However, he primarily achieved this supremacy by means of the army (Chapter 6). And it is with a good deal of justice that he has been described as the creator of the 'military monarchy'. That was a lesson Septimius had learnt in a hard school, because he only attained, and stayed upon, the imperial throne at all because he had put down his predecessor and several rivals – by military force. This taught him that to be an emperor required him to have, and control, a powerful army. So that is the principal keynote of the period. It is a Roman empire in which the emperor dominates events not through the senate or any other organ of the state, but by means of the soldiers.

They, whether members of the praetorian guard or legionaries, were nowadays very often not Italians but provincials (Chapters 5, 6). Here is another keynote of the period. Septimius Severus himself originated from Africa, and his wife and subsequent emperors came from Syria. We are witnessing the rise of the provinces and of provincials (Chapter 5). This must not be overstressed because Rome was still the ruler of the world. But the provinces, especially Africa and Syria, were taking giant steps towards equalling Italy as dominant regions of the Roman empire.

In addition, however, Septimius suffered from a grave handicap, and made a serious mistake, if not two. His handicap was his health. This ceased to be good after he had been stricken with smallpox in Egypt in the middle of his reign, though it is not clear that this was what caused the permanent deterioration of his health. He was such a very active man by nature, and the subsequent weakness of his legs and feet, whatever it was due to (Chapter 3), must have caused him irritation and embarrassment.

But his great mistake was to think that his two sons, Caracalla and Geta, must become his heirs. He justified this duality on historical grounds, and what happened later to the empire – that is to say, the division into two parts, in AD 364 – shows that he was not far wrong. However, Caracalla hated Geta and murdered him (Chapter 4). It seems surprising to us today that such an able man as Septimius had so blind a spot that he believed his older son Caracalla could be an adequate heir and successor. But dynastic feelings of this sort went back a long way, and one must also ascribe to Septimius a very human belief in his son, for all his obvious faults. For Septimius's second mistake he can hardly be blamed. By force of arms, he wore down Parthia in the east (Chapter 5) to such an extent that by the end of our period it had been superseded by the far more dangerous Persians. But it would scarcely have been possible for Septimius to guard against this eventual outcome in an area beyond his control.

Two other features of the period deserve special notice. One is the prominence of women (Chapter 8). Septimius's wife Julia Domna was clearly a remarkable person. She did not, however, rule the empire, because her very powerful husband did that. But her sister Julia Maesa and her niece Julia Mamaea did, after that, control the Roman world. It was an age, that is to say, in which the greater part of the civilized world was ruled by women. This had never happened before, to the same extent, though it is somewhat unexpected to hear this. It is unexpected because we read so much more about Messalina and the two Agrippinas in the first century AD, since they were written about by brilliant historians and biographers. Julia Maesa and the others were not. Yet they possessed immense and unprecedented power. Another significant feature of the period is the increased prominence, and prolific production, of the lawyers (Chapter 9). Most other writers, except a novelist (Chapter 10), were pretty poor (Appendix) – if that had not been the case with the historians, we should know more about what went on. But the lawyers were excellent, and of immense importance to the future.

The Severan age can also be viewed in terms of money. Indeed the same could be said about any period of the Roman empire. Everything depended upon how much money the emperors could manage to get their hands on. But this situation became especially dramatic and pressing in the time of Septimius Severus. He inherited a treasury which had been almost emptied by the ludicrous excesses of Commodus. And yet, in spite of Septimius's own heavy expenditure, for example in putting down his Roman and other enemies, he left the coffers very fully equipped with money when he died; even though the emperors of the period had to lay hands on much more money than ever before, not only because of the need to suppress numerous enemies and usurpers, but because of the gigantic and greatly increased cost of the army at all times.

How Septimius raised all these funds will be discussed below (Chapter 7). But in any case his inadequate successors frittered it all away. However, Julia Mamaea, the mother of Severus Alexander (Chapter 8), was accused of meanness – because of her recognition of the need to cut down expenses. And it was, indeed, remarkable that the régimes of this period just managed to keep their heads above water from a financial point of view. The imperial collapse did not occur until later.

Three more points need to be made about what we may call the 'Severan' period, AD 193–235. First of all, it was an age of novel-readers, and witnessed the life and writing of one of the greatest novelists of all time (Longus: Chapter 10; cf. also above). Secondly, this epoch, or at least its earlier half, was a great period of building (Chapter 11). At Rome itself, the imposing Arch of Septimius Severus and the immense Baths of Caracalla are still ample testimonies to this achievement. And there are many remarkable remains in the provinces, notably in north Africa, which bear further witness to enormous activities in this field. Moreover, fine building was equalled by magnificent portraiture, especially of the emperors and their family.

Monotheistic religion, too, had gained ground to an extraordinary extent. When one says this, one thinks of course first of Christianity, whose writer Tertullian possessed immense authority and power (Chapter 12). But it is also necessary to recognize that the pagan, monotheistic worship of the Sun, despite the excesses of Elagabalus in importing a Syrian version of the cult, had become very widely practised; and that the Olympian deities tended increasingly to be regarded as appendages or manifestations of this all-powerful deity. The effort to set up Apollonius of Tyana (near Niğde, Lycaonia) as a supreme pagan exemplar – even if, as is now thought, this was done as a deliberate counterpoise to Jesus Christ – was not a lasting success. But, all the same, there was a great deal of pagan monotheism

(Chapter 12); though the monotheism of the future lay increasingly in the hands of the Christians.

At a wider level, we have come to a juncture when the early Roman empire had ended, and the full regimentation of later times, after a period of collapse and reorganization, was at hand. In the whole of this process the reigns of Septimius Severus and his successors were decisive. The Roman world had changed.

I am happy to offer acknowledgements for the help I have received from Richard Stoneman, Caroline Cautley and Victoria Peters of Routledge; from Professor T. V. Buttrey; from the cartographer Henry Kim; from the staff of Alinari, Florence; and from my wife. I also owe specific acknowledgements to the following for quotations I have included from their works: E. Cary, translation of Dio, *Roman History*, Vol. IX (Harvard, 1927); E. C. Echols, translation of Herodian, *Herodian of Antioch's History of the Roman Empire* (University of California Press, 1961); N. Holzberg, *The Ancient Novel* (Routledge, 1995); A. W. Lawrence, *Classical Sculpture* (Cape, 1929); P. Levi, *A History of Greek Literature* (Viking, 1985); J. R. Morgan in J. R. Morgan and R. Stoneman (eds), *Greek Fiction* (Routledge, 1994); J. M. C. Toynbee, *The Art of the Romans* (Thames & Hudson, 1965); J. B. Ward-Perkins, *Roman Imperial Architecture* (Penguin, 1981).

Michael Grant
Gattaiola, 1995

1

SEPTIMIUS SEVERUS AND THE STRUGGLE FOR POWER

Lucius Septimius Severus, who was emperor from 193 to 211, had greater difficulty than anyone before him in seizing the throne. There was a certain resemblance between 193 and 69, when the Julio-Claudian house had come to an end and there had been civil wars. But this time it was even worse, and the task of Septimius Severus was severer than Vespasian's (69–79). It was, indeed, a remarkable feat that Septimius succeeded in reaching the throne at all. He did so by putting down not only the transient emperor who came before him, Didius Julianus, but by suppressing two formidable rivals, Pescennius Niger and Clodius Albinus.

Septimius Severus (Plates 3–4) had been born in 145 at Lepcis Magna (Lebda) in Tripolitana. He was given the name of his paternal grandfather, who was probably a man of Carthaginian (Punic) origin (perhaps with some Berber blood), and had migrated from Lepcis Magna to Italy in the last years of the first century AD, achieving promotion to equestrian (knightly) status. Septimius's mother Fulvia Pia may have come from an Italian family which moved to north Africa.[1]

Septimius became a member of the Roman senate (perhaps in about 173), held the governorships of Gallia Lugdunensis and Sicily, and was then consul (190) and governor of Upper Pannonia. After the short reign of Pertinax in 193, followed by the accession of Didius Julianus, Septimius was proclaimed emperor by his legions (see n. 4), apparently at Carnuntum (Petronell) – or possibly at Savaria (Szombathely), also in Upper Pannonia – while Pescennius Niger received a similar salutation in the east.

After granting the title of Caesar to Clodius Albinus, governor of Britain, Septimius set out for the east against this rival claimant, Pescennius Niger. Decisive victories over Pescennius Niger were followed by punitive expeditions against the Osrhoeni and other Parthian vassals who had helped Niger. Before returning to Europe to fight against Albinus, Septimius raised his son Caracalla to the rank of Caesar in Albinus's place and adopted himself into the family of the Antonines (196).

The issue against Albinus was settled in a battle near Lugdunum (Lyon) (February 197). After a short stay in Rome, Septimius moved east to retaliate against Parthia for its at least verbal support of Niger. A campaign culminated in the fall of Ctesiphon (perhaps in December 197). After two abortive attacks on the desert fortress of Hatra (Al-Hadr) the war ended with the annexation of Osrhoene and Mesopotamia by the Romans (199). The next two years were spent by Septimius in Syria and Egypt. On 1 January 202 he and his elder son Caracalla became joint consuls at Antioch. Then Septimius and his family returned to Rome. Septimius spent much of the next six years in Italy, but visited Africa in 203–5, and perhaps in 208 as well. In 208 he set out with his wife and two sons, Caracalla and Geta, for Britain. In the hope of intimidating the Caledonians Scotland was invaded. The Roman losses, however, were severe, and a temporary peace was patched up in the summer of 210. Worn out by sickness and broken in spirit by Caracalla's unfilial conduct, which consorted badly with intentions of founding a dynasty, Septimius died at Eburacum (York) in 211.

How much should he be regarded as an African?[2] Opinions differ. Did he have an African accent? Probably; his sister spoke with one, and he had, as we saw, some Punic (if not Berber) blood. Was he dark-skinned, or more dark-skinned than the Italians? John Malalas says he was. But we cannot be sure. There is a tendency nowadays to say that the *Africitas* of Septimius has been over-estimated. Yet it was from Africa that he came (Plate 4), and this influenced his attitude towards Italy (Chapter 5).

Something more must be said about Septimius's accession. He had been hailed emperor as soon as the news of the succession of Didius Julianus arrived, and took the name of Pertinax in honour of that emperor's predecessor. Septimius had, locally, administered the oath of allegiance to Pertinax.[3] It was on the accession of Didius Julianus, with the support of nearly all the Danubian and Rhenish legions,[4] that Septimius made his dash for Rome, where he spent thirty days in June (from the 2nd) and early July of 193 – between three and four months after his initial proclamation. It seems very possible that Pertinax had intended him to be his heir.[5]

But Septimius's claim to the imperial throne was contested by Pescennius Niger in the east, for which Septimius left promptly in order to deal with him. Gaius Pescennius Niger was born in about AD 135 (or a little later), and came from an Italian family of equestrian (knightly) rank.[6] Promoted into the senate by Commodus, he fought against the Sarmatians in Dacia in 183, and became consul. Then, in 190, he was appointed to the governorship of Syria, where his lavish output on public entertainments made him popular. When he obtained news, in 193, of the assassination of Pertinax and the problems that were besetting Didius Julianus, he allowed himself to be proclaimed emperor by his soldiers at Antioch – at approximately the time of Septimius Severus's proclamation in Upper Pannonia. (Like Septimius, he had probably already intended to seize the throne once Pertinax was out of the way.) The character of Pescennius Niger has been disputed. Discipline and austerity are ascribed to him. But it is plausible to agree that he was neither particularly good nor particularly bad, although we have, of course, mainly his victorious enemy's account.[7]

All the nine legions stationed in the east declared for Niger. And he gained the support (though no troops, for internal reasons) of King Vologases V of Parthia (cf. above; and Chapter 5). Within Europe, too, Niger obtained the allegiance of Byzantium – the later Constantinople (Istanbul) – and intended to occupy another city, Perinthus (Marmaraereğlisi, Ereğli), to ensure him the control of the main land routes. But Septimius Severus, arriving from Rome, sent ahead an advance guard which captured Perinthus. And then he proceeded to besiege Byzantium. Niger's commander-in-chief, Asellius Aemilianus, was defeated across the Bosphorus near Cyzicus (Balkiz) and again in the neighbourhood of Nicaea (Iznik), in the narrow passes west of the city.[8] With what was left of his army Niger withdrew eastwards across the Taurus (Toros) mountains. However, his rearguard was swept aside by the enemy, who broke through the Cilician Gates (Külek Boğazi), endangering Antioch itself. In order to stop their advance Pescennius Niger moved forward to Issus (Deli Çay), on the borders of Syria and Asia Minor. Nevertheless, his army was again defeated there.[9] He returned to Antioch. But when news came that Septimius was not far away he evacuated the city and fled eastwards towards the Euphrates. Before Pescennius Niger was able to cross the river, however, he was overtaken and killed (195). Byzantium, discouraged, surrendered. Its siege had lasted for more than two years: the city seems to have fallen late in 195, perhaps in December, although an earlier month is not out of the question.

Pescennius Niger had been distinctly popular at Rome, which caused Septimius particular worry. Niger's coins of various eastern mints,[10] in addition to displaying eastern themes, show that he had intended to inaugurate a new Golden Age, linked with Augustus. His key title was 'Justus' – indicating straight and faithful dealing: though how far this was translated into action we cannot tell. It is probably fair enough to conclude that Septimius won the war against him by taking advantage of Pescennius Niger's military mistakes. After that fight was over Septimius embarked on the First Parthian War (Chapter 5), partly in order to suppress Barsemius of Hatra, who (like Parthia, it was said: cf. above), had supported Pescennius Niger.

But when Septimius came back to Rome – as we learn from the coins that he did – a sinister incident occurred when the populace 'indulged in the most open lamentations' (about the imminent war against Albinus, governor of Britain).

> There had assembled . . . an untold multitude and they had watched the chariots racing . . . without applauding, as was their custom, any of the contestants at all. But when these races were over and the charioteers were about to begin another event, they first enjoined silence upon one another and then suddenly all clapped their hands at the same moment and also joined in a shout, praying for good fortune for the public welfare.
>
> This was what they first cried out. Then, applying the terms 'Queen' and 'Immortal' to Rome, they shouted: 'How long are we to suffer such things?' and 'How long are we to be waging war?' . . .
>
> This demonstration was one thing that increased our apprehensions still more.

That was said by a Senator, Dio Cassius (Appendix) but it increased the apprehensions of Septimius Severus to an even greater degree. It was, for him, a nightmare come true. The emperors were always afraid of trouble from the people of Rome – hence their repeated acts of generosity towards the metropolitan population (Chapter 7). Indeed, they feared, very often, that these people would bring them down: though in this they were wrong, because it was usually the army that did so. Perhaps that was because the emperors treated the civilian populace of Rome so generously. Or, more probably, the fear was just unwarranted. This demonstration against Septimius Severus may well, as Dio Cassius and other ancient historians hint, have been organized and orchestrated by the supporters of Clodius Albinus in the city, who were numerous, not least in the senate.

Nevertheless, at about the turn of the year, Septimius broke with Albinus, whether unwillingly or deliberately we cannot tell,[11] and left Rome to contest his claim to the imperial throne.

Clodius Albinus (Decimus Clodius Septimius Albinus) was probably born between 140 and 150. He was said to have come from a rich (noble?) family of Hadrumetum (Sousse) in north Africa, but this remains doubtful. He seems to have started his official career as an *eques* (knight). But he became a member of the senate during the later years of Marcus Aurelius, to whom, as governor of Bithynia-Pontus, he remained loyal during the rebellion of Avidius Cassius in 175. Thereafter Albinus fought in Dacia (182–4), and may have been governor of Upper or Lower Germany. Consul around the year 190, he then obtained the governorship of Britain, where he had to deal with a turbulent garrison.[12]

Septimius Severus, when he claimed to be the successor of Didius Julianus in 193, freed his hands for the imminent war against his eastern rival Pescennius Niger by declaring Clodius Albinus to be Caesar. This title implied that he was destined to be Septimius's successor. And the coinage of the time makes it clear that this was so.[13] It might seem somewhat naive of Albinus to have trusted, apparently, the authenticity of this offer and to have, in consequence, accepted the offer, and thus, in 194, to have obtained a second consulship *in absentia*, keeping quiet for two years – although Septimius had two sons, Caracalla and Geta, whom he presumably intended, when they became old enough, to become his successors. However, Caracalla was at this stage only 5 years old, and Geta was even younger. And Clodius Albinus, whatever his doubts about Septimius's motives, could well have hoped that he himself might become emperor if Septimius was defeated and killed in his forthcoming war against Pescennius Niger.

But it was Niger who was defeated and killed, and so Septimius survived. In 195 the relationship between him and Albinus was broken off (so that Caracalla became Caesar instead). In consequence Albinus, abandoning his allegiance to Septimius, had himself proclaimed Augustus, and was declared an enemy of the state by Septimius's government. Yet Albinus's cause was by no means hopeless. Not only had he, as we saw, many supporters at Rome, but he was also backed, for example, by the governor of Hispania Tarraconensis, Lucius Novius Rufus. It is not impossible that Albinus planned to march into Italy. For if he remained inactive, disaster was sure to follow, and he did not intend that this should happen.

So he sailed from Britain across the English channel, and set up his capital, for the time being, at Lugdunum (Lyon). But he failed to secure the support of the legions on the Rhine, and could not, as he may have wished, invade Italy, because the Alpine passes were blocked by the troops of Septimius. The latter, on the other hand, arrived in Gaul (196–7). And then, after an initial battle at Tinurtium (Tournus), which went in his favour, he decisively defeated Albinus in a huge confrontation near Lugdunum (February 197).

Various important points emerge from this story of the war between Septimius Severus and Clodius Albinus. First, it is noteworthy that, faced with the earlier war against Pescennius Niger, Septimius had made Albinus his Caesar – a fact that is confirmed by the coins. The reason why Albinus accepted this obviously dishonest offer has already been discussed. And its withdrawal corresponded with, and probably in large part caused, the rebellion of Albinus, whose self-declaration as Augustus is once again announced by the coinage – this time, his own. Secondly, Septimius had now had to fight hard, and extremely expensively (Chapter 7), on two fronts, in addition to his original march on Rome, in order to sustain his position (it was fortunate that there were no German attacks at the time). This had several effects. One was that he noted the names of many leading Romans who had taken sides, or been prepared to take sides, against him. After his victory over Albinus and arrival in Rome early in June 197, he conducted a blood-bath against these enemies and potential enemies in Rome[14] - as well as in Gaul – and confiscated their properties (he had not taken similar action against the supporters of Pescennius Niger).

This was a significant point, because the campaigns, in east and west, had cost a great deal of money, which was to a considerable extent recuperated by these confiscations (cf. Chapter 7). Another lasting effect of the civil wars was Septimius's enormous reliance on the army (Chapter 6) – which had pulled him through – in contrast to his distaste for the senate, which had spawned so much of the opposition. He gave early evidence of this distaste by a ferocious speech, in which he praised the ruthlessness of Augustus, Marius and Sulla.[15]

So Septimius had won, and had become emperor. It had been a savagely hard-fought struggle. He had not won because of any military genius, because that was not what he possessed. In fact, he was the least military of the various contenders, and could instead be described as something of a bureaucrat. And yet he moved his troops about with speed and decisiveness, and he was intellectually energetic to a remarkable degree. Indeed, he was exceptionally able, as well as conscientious and hard-working – and in addition, well-versed in Greek and Latin literature,[16] despite whatever degree of *Africitas* may be attributed to him (see above).

He was also harsh, cruel, vindictive and rather arrogant. It is a pity that his autobiography is lost, although of course it would only have stressed his favourable side. He seems to have been abnormally superstitious, and addicted to horoscopes, and was said to have regarded himself as predestined to rule. But he caught smallpox in Egypt, and for the rest of his reign suffered from bad feet – though it is difficult to attribute this to smallpox – which limited his physical activity (see also above).

2

THE PRAETORIANS AND THEIR PREFECTS: PLAUTIANUS

In 193, before moving against Pescennius Niger, Septimius Severus had already taken a decisive step by cashiering and replacing the praetorian guard. This, it was said, was how it happened.

> He quietly sent private letters to the tribunes and centurions, promising them rich rewards if they would persuade the praetorians in Rome to submit and obey the emperor's orders. He also sent an open letter to the praetorian camp, directing the soldiers to leave their weapons behind in the camps and to come forth unarmed, as was the custom when they escorted the emperor to the sacrifices or to the celebration of a festival . . .
>
> Trusting these orders and persuaded by their tribunes, the praetorians left their arms behind and appeared from the camp in holiday uniform, carrying laurel branches . . . Then, at a given signal, they were all seized while cheering him in unison . . . Severus ordered his troops to hold the praetorians in a tight ring of steel . . .
>
> When he had them netted like fish in his circle of weapons, like prisoners of war, the enraged emperor shouted in a loud voice: . . . 'Helpless and prostrate, you lie before us now, victims of our might . . . You murdered your revered and benevolent old emperor [Pertinax], whom it was your sworn duty to protect . . . I order the soldiers who have you surrounded to cashier you, to strip off any military uniform or equipment you are wearing, and to drive you off naked. And I order you to get yourselves as far from the city of Rome as is humanly possible.'[1]

Indeed, that is what seems to have been the outcome: in sharp

14

contrast to the large increases in pay that they had been promised by Didius Julianus (Chapters 6, 7),[2] the praetorians were now instructed to betake themselves more than a hundred miles away from the capital. This was, at the outset, a popular move, because the guard had been violent and offensive to the civilian population. But it did not by any means signify that the unit had come to an end. On the contrary, it was immediately revived and increased in size, to ten cohorts of double strength[3] – designed to be a sort of strategic reserve, along with the legions that were now posted at Albanum near Rome (Chapter 5 and n. 2). This legion created a certain counterpoise to the praetorians' power, which was, however, still very considerable.

Moreover, the composition of the guard was now to be different. It was to consist no longer of Romans and Italians – who did not mind this exclusion, for the most part, since they had become increasingly unwilling to undertake military service. Instead, the guard was to be composed of men drafted from the crack Danubian or Rhenish legions; although that put an end to the popularity of Septimius's change, since these Illyrian soldiers were disliked at Rome. Nevertheless, he gave the new guardsmen constant and excessive donatives, and raised their pay considerably (from 1,250 to 1,700 *denarii*; cf. Chapter 7) (moreover, they, or a good mass of them, probably accompanied Septimius when he went to Britain). Caracalla substantially increased the guardsmen's pay once again (212).[4]

They preferred Severus Alexander to his predecessor, Elagabalus – who had made a joke about his unpopularity with them.[5] But none the less they became dissatisfied with Severus Alexander as well, killing their super-prefect Ulpian (Chapter 9): although the emperor's mother Julia Mamaea (Chapter 8) had from the start claimed to be their benefactor, and asserted that the money which she had amassed was intended for them. But meanwhile the praetorians were losing ground to the legions,[6] and the real end of the guard came on the death of Severus Alexander, when there emerged in his place the first legionary to become emperor (Maximinus I).

Another of the outstanding features of the period was the increased importance of the guard's commander, the praetorian prefect.

This tendency reached its climax under Septimius Severus, when the prefect Gaius Fulvius Plautianus became immensely powerful.[7] It was remarkable that a ruler with the dominant personality of Septimius, at the height of his strength and capacity, became as completely reliant on a praetorian prefect as any emperor before him. This was because the burdens of running so vast and complex an empire were beyond the powers of any one man. Tiberius (AD 14–37) had felt the same, and had employed Sejanus. The man whom Septimius selected to share his own duties, although allegedly annoyed by the man's grandeur, was his fellow-African, and indeed fellow-townsman, Plautianus.

After taking over the praetorian prefecture in AD 197 – when he was probably left in charge at Rome, and murdered his fellow-prefects – Plautianus had become a senator, and came to exert an autocratic set of powers, pervading nearly every aspect of government, including taxation and the supply of grain. Furthermore, his 14–year-old daughter Plautilla was married to the emperor's elder son, Caracalla. Whether the marriage was consummated or not, it cannot have been much fun for her, since although she was said to be pretty disagreeable he was little short of appalling.

However, after Plautianus had been practically in charge of the empire for more than seven years (and his great riches caused popular anger), the emperor's brother (Lucius Septimius Geta), on his death-bed, provided information that damned him. It evidently related to an alleged plot by Plautianus to take over the imperial position.[8] But Plautianus had, in any case, become the enemy of the empress Julia Domna (Chapter 8),[9] and was also greatly disliked by Caracalla, whose marriage to his daughter Plautilla was far from happy.[10]

And so, eventually, Caracalla arranged for three centurions to assert that they and seven others had been told by Plautianus to kill both Septimius and Caracalla. Accordingly, in their presence, Plautianus was struck down and murdered, on the grounds that he had given these orders. The fatal deed perhaps took place on 22 January 205. And Plautilla followed him into ruin (recorded by the removal of her face and name from official monuments).[11] As for Septimius, he improved his own financial position by confiscating the dead man's wealth and incorporating it in his *res privata* (Chapter 7); and Plautianus's statues were melted down.

When Plautianus fell, he was succeeded by joint praetorian prefects, one of whom was the outstanding jurist Papinian (Chapter 9). During the period that initially followed, the military authority of the praetorian prefects tended to be restricted. However, they retained and even increased their civilian duties and powers. In particular, they not only had a Council of their own, but served as the ruler's personal deputies on *his* imperial Council. And – no doubt with some indebtedness to Septimius's own strong interest in the law (Chapter 9) – their judicial powers were amplified, so that, beyond the hundredth milestone from Rome, they became the supreme criminal judges in Italy, if they had not been before: quite an important task at that time, when there was a great deal of brigandage, encouraged by the exclusion of Italians from the praetorian guard (so that some of them became bandits instead), and exemplified by the widespread activities of the brigand leader Bulla Felix (206–7), who drew extensively, also, on deserters. One way and another, it was useful for the prefects to be lawyers: although the custom lapsed owing to the murder of the super-prefect Ulpian (Chapter 9), after whose death, in the reign of Severus Alexander, it was decided that jurists could not control the guard, and the prefects had better be military men, as they had often been before.

3

THE GESTURES OF SEPTIMIUS

While still in the east, in 195, soon after his first 'victory' over the Parthians (Chapter 5), Septimius Severus had taken a remarkable, dishonest step. That is to say, he had announced his 'adoption' into the family of Marcus Aurelius, of whom he asserted that he was the son. This unprecedented posthumous move indicated a claim to legitimate succession, and stressed the divine superiority of the continuing, lasting imperial house (possibly under the Syrian influence of his wife Julia Domna; Chapter 8).[1]

And Septimius's sonship of Marcus Aurelius implied brotherhood to Commodus, who was now deified. Those who had dutifully vilified Commodus now had, rather embarrassingly, to eat their words.[2] An inscription gives a complete list of the Antonine ancestors whom Septimius thus allegedly acquired.[3] For a short time, he called himself DIVI M. PII F(*ilius*) (son of the deified Aurelius Pius).

As for his elder son Caracalla (born in 189), he was not only made Caesar in place of Clodius Albinus (Chapter 1), but had previously been given the name Antoninus,[4] by which name the army acclaimed him in the year of his Caesarship, 196: as the *Historia Augusta* (Appendix) remarked, 'the name of Antoninus was at that time so greatly beloved that he who had not the prestige of this name did not seem to merit the imperial power'.[5]

So Caracalla was now destined to be Septimius's principal heir and successor.[6] This was a poor decision – especially with the precedent of Commodus's succession to his father Marcus Aurelius to look back upon. But Septimius no doubt justified it on the grounds that dynastic succession and strength were what the empire (as well as he himself) needed. He was also presumably influenced by a father's personal support of his elder son, whom he loved more than he loved his country. Caracalla, therefore, was pushed forward in

18

every possible way, and indeed, for a large part of the reign (from 198), he became, despite his youth, joint Augustus and full emperor as a colleague of his now ailing father; although Septimius was apparently not unconscious of his son's inadequacies, which he is said to have stressed before his death on 9 February 211.

Caracalla possessed the character of his father (whom, it was said, he at least once intended to kill; cf. next chapter) in exaggerated and perhaps mentally deranged form. His famous portrait (Plate 12; Chapter 11) does not lie, or minimize his defects. He showed cruelty and vindictiveness, and was believed to be cowardly as well. His health, like his father's, was poor:[7] hence he, quite as much as, or even more than, Septimius, was keen on the cult of the health-god Aesculapius. His desire to ape Alexander the Great aimed too high, and did him no good (even if, as is now supposed, it did not have much effect on his eastern plans). He was known as 'Caracallus' because he wore a Gallic robe of that name, a hooded great-coat. But on coins and inscriptions he appears as Marcus Aurelius Antoninus.

One reason for pushing Caracalla forward was the bad health which increasingly engulfed Septimius (even if, as we saw, Caracalla too was unwell). There is something to be said, as we have seen, for the view that the smallpox Septimius caught in Egypt permanently affected him. Later on, however, it was his feet that gave him trouble (Chapter 1). When he entered Rome in 202, he could not stand in his triumphal chariot because they hurt him so much – and his son Caracalla was voted a triumph on behalf of his father. Subsequently, in Britain, Septimius had to be carried in a covered litter (and the harsh climate of the country certainly cannot have done him any good). Either he had gout – which was said, in general, to be due to over-indulgence,[8] although Septimius was not accused of this – or he suffered from arthritis. His death was apparently foreseen. However, long before he died, his poor health must have conflicted seriously with his mental alertness and desire for vigorous activity, which his earlier physical toughness had facilitated.

So that was one of the reasons why Caracalla was so vehemently promoted. There was to be a Severan dynasty, or rather, fictitiously, a continuation of the Antonine dynasty. Septimius had made one mistake by bringing forward Caracalla. But he compounded this, although he may well have meant to mitigate it, by bringing forward his younger son Geta as well. Geta (Plates 8, 9), whose character is uncertain (since he lost; cf. next Chapter), probably became Caesar at the same time as Caracalla was made Augustus, and he was destined to become joint emperor with Caracalla (as he did for a very short time).[9] The idea of a dual rulership, which Severus stressed, was derived from the joint reign of Marcus Aurelius and Lucius Verus. However, it is strange that Septimius did not see that under Caracalla and Geta it was completely unworkable. If his British expedition, as has been said, was an effort to reconcile the two young men to one another, the effort did not succeed. As Septimius is supposed to have recognized on his death-bed, they hated each other, and could not possibly get on.[10]

4

THE SUCCESSORS

Caracalla was not only hot-tempered and cruel, as the makers of his portrait-busts show all too clearly (cf. above), but he was also said to be slack about his legal duties, and indeed, according to some reports, negligent about his domestic administration in general, which he willingly left to his mother Julia Domna (Chapter 8) (who had originally insisted on his promotion, so it was believed),[1] while he was away commanding armies in the east.

He was also said not only to have arranged the murder of Plautianus (Chapter 2) but to have intended to assassinate his own father Septimius Severus, who, as we saw in the last chapter, was conscious of his defects, while at the same time continuing to advance him. But we must remember that a lot of the hostile tradition that has come down to us was due to Dio Cassius (see Appendix), who, like other writers with senatorial sympathies, hated Caracalla, while he himself, it was also asserted, seemed quite happy to insult senators. On the other side, it does seem possible that the rude remarks about Caracalla's administrative and judicial activities are untrue, or at least exaggerated, and that, instead, although in dubious health, he was pretty methodical, as well as eager to be kept properly informed. He was undoubtedly popular with the soldiers. They liked his high-spirited affability, and his frugal readiness to share their burdens, and indeed his preference for their company over that of others. He was not, it is true, much of a military commander, yet he was something of a strategist all the same, with an eye for fortresses and defensive positions.

After the death of Septimius Severus on 4 February 211, both Caracalla and Geta hastened back to Rome, where they arrived in May, and lived in separate quarters: until Caracalla, who was predominantly in charge, had Geta assassinated (allegedly in their mother's arms), perhaps in January or February 212. A holocaust of Geta's supporters followed – 20,000 of them were said to have lost their lives – and his face was erased from reliefs and his name from inscriptions, while dramatists avoided referring to any character of the same name in their plays.[2] After the murder of Geta, Caracalla felt nervous that the dead man might have been popular among the praetorians, and consequently gave them an enormous largesse, never forgetting, as his father had apparently enjoined him, to enrich the army (cf. Chapters 6, 7).

Caracalla's reign (211–17) was mostly spent fighting in the east – as we shall see later (Chapter 5). This was what he preferred, since he was in the company of the soldiers. He left the task of administering the empire to his mother Julia Domna (Chapter 8).

The senator Dio Cassius, as we saw, described Caracalla's tenure of the throne as disastrous. However, he is thought to have carried on his father's strong government. He increased the criminal powers of provincial governors, but unlike Septimius did not allow the imperial Council much freedom. Caracalla did not hold any consulship after 213. Probably he regarded the office as too Republican for his autocratic temperament.

Then on 8 April 217, while on the way to do honour to the deity Lunus (the Moon),[3] the centre of whose worship was at Carrhae (Altibasak), he was murdered, at the age of 29. Supposedly he was stabbed to death while getting off his horse to relieve himself. The prompter of his assassination, and his successor from 217 to 218, was Macrinus.

Macrinus (Marcus Opellius), emperor from 217 to 218,[4] had been born in 164 at Caesarea (Iol) in Mauretania Caesariensis, where his family was poor and undistinguished. As a youth, we are told, he worked successively as a gladiator, a huntsman and a postal courier. Then he proceeded to Rome, where he operated as a jurist, becoming the legal adviser of Septimius's praetorian prefect Plautianus, who was murdered in 205. Subsequently Macrinus was director of traffic on the Via Flaminia and administrator of Septimius's private properties. In 212 Caracalla made him joint praetorian prefect, and in 216 Macrinus participated in the Parthian expedition of the emperor, who in the following year arranged that he should have consular status (*ornamenta consularia*). During that spring, however, he found out that a message denouncing him as a security risk had been dispatched (supposedly by an astrologer) to Caracalla, whom

Macrinus consequently caused to be killed, on 8 April. After a series of intrigues the soldiers then declared Macrinus himself emperor in Caracalla's place (Plate 15).

Conservatives held it against him that he was not only the first Mauretanian but also the first non-senator to occupy the imperial throne, although Macrinus tactfully apologized for his non-senatorial origins and met with some approval from the senators because they had so greatly disliked Caracalla. Yet he owed his appointment as emperor entirely to the army, whose support of him, however, might well not last, as he was aware, especially if his dominant role in the assassination of Caracalla – whom they liked – became known. So he arranged for Caracalla's deification (see below, n. 9). But even so he rapidly lost the favour of the soldiers.[5]

In common with many other leading people of the era who came to sticky ends, the qualities of Macrinus were not agreed upon by the ancient writers. Was he harsh and tyrannical, or a man of good character and useful experience? Certainly he was not ungenerous with largesses of grain (though not of money).[6] But even if careful not to assume a consulship at once, he caused offence in influential quarters by merely notifiying the senate of his accession without applying to it for the post. Furthermore, he was badly received by the Roman population in the Circus. This was a sign of the fact that, displaying, as he did, a lack of sense of purpose or appearance of activity, he failed to gain the support of public opinion, as well as increasingly lacking military support. As for the latter point, it was unwise of him, if he wanted to keep the army quiet, to stay so long at Antioch – which he did partly because he feared a renewed invasion from the Parthians, whom he treated, according to Dio Cassius, with too much humiliating indulgence; although not everyone agreed.[7]

Like Septimius, Macrinus aspired to found a dynasty. With this in mind, and in the hope of appeasing the troops, he made his own son Diadumenian (born in 204) first Caesar and Antoninus[8] (with an extensive largesse from himself to the troops at the same time) and then joint Augustus. But this did not help Macrinus, all the same. Nor did his own tactful deification (to please the praetorians and other soldiers) of Caracalla, whom he had murdered[9] – or his employment of the name Severus, or his revision of his own portrait-style on his coins, to make himself look more impressive. The fact that he was not a senator was against Macrinus, and so, of course, was his loss of favour with the soldiery, whom he ought to have cut down in size, instead of reducing their pay to save money.

But his most fatal mistake was to send all three Syrian women – the sister and nieces of Septimius's wife Julia Domna, who had committed suicide – back to their home town of Emesa (Homs) in Syria, with the two sons of the younger ladies. The women were Julia Maesa (widow of a former consul Julius Avitus, Plate 21), and her daughters Julia Soaemias (wife of a fellow-Syrian Sextus Marius Marcellus, who after a successful career as a knight (eques) had been promoted to senatorial status), and Julia Mamaea. The boys were Elagabalus (the son of Soaemias) and Severus Alexander (the son of Mamaea).

It was all of these, with the help of their extensive funds, who caused the downfall of Macrinus, after what was regarded as his meanness to the army and a humiliating peace with Parthia (see n. 7). The fatal clash between the forces of Macrinus and his Roman and Syrian enemies took place in a battle twenty-four miles east of Antioch, on 8 June 218. Julia Maesa's general Gannys of Emesa – supposedly the lover of Julia Soaemias – who was in command of the Roman army in Syria (the headquarters of the Legio III Gallica was not far off) proved victorious, and Macrinus and Diadumenian lost their lives.

The new emperor was the son of Julia Soaemias, Varius Avitus Bassianus, commonly known as Elagabalus.[10] He duly called himself Marcus Aurelius Antoninus, his grandmother Julia Maesa having declared that he was the son of Caracalla, who had been similarly named (Plates 16–18; cf. n. 11 below).

Elagabalus had been born in 204, and was emperor from 218 to 222. It was Julia Domna's sister Julia Maesa who had decided to get rid of Macrinus. He had requested her, as he saw, to withdraw to her home at Emesa in Syria. But this town, and the soldiery stationed in Syria, gave her a suitable base for a revolt. The 14-year-old son of her daughter Julia Soaemias, whom we know as Elagabalus, occupied the hereditary priesthood of the Sun-god El-gabal (an offshoot of the principal Semitic god El) at Emesa. He possessed a striking personal beauty which meant that he contributed spectacular picturesqueness to the elaborate, jewel-encrusted ritual of his cult.

Elagabalus, like Macrinus, merely notified the senators of his accession. They agreed, for fear of the soldiers. And so the new emperor entered Rome, in spring, or July or September, 219. To avoid any suggestion that his origins were exotic, he took and stressed the name of Antoninus, claiming, as was stated, to be the son of Caracalla (to impress the soldiers).[11] Yet he never became very Roman. And his short reign was a joke, and a bad joke at that. Elagabalus was a passive homosexual, and the historians' pages are full of obscene stories about his life. The trouble was that he was extremely young, and saw no reason not to indulge his sexual tendencies to the full. There were, fortunately, practically no important political or military events during those four years. All we need to note is that the young emperor, dressed up in eastern robes as a priest, was sincere about his religion but very wasteful of money. Being so youthful, he was under the control of Julia Soaemias, who, however, proved unhelpful about curbing his irregular tendencies – distraught, as she surely was, by the disappearance of Gannys, now the praetorian prefect, who was assassinated.

Anyway, owing to Elagabalus's behaviour, Julia Soaemias's mother Julia Maesa had to step in to prevent the imperial family from falling into total disrepute. On the excuse that Elagabalus must be left free to carry out his religious duties, she persuaded him (with the senate's approval) to adopt his cousin Severus Alexander as his son[12] – although he made fun of the occasion, saying that his new 'son' was already 12 years old.[13] The new praetorian prefect, Comazon Eutychianus, was not a great help. But Julia Maesa tried to make her grandson, the emperor, look respectable by arranging for him to marry at least three successive wives, Julia Paula, Aquilia Severa and Annia Faustina, all of whom, in turn, appeared on coins (for Aquilia Severa see Plate 20).

Indeed, he married Aquilia Severa twice. But his association with her caused a scandal, because she was one of the Vestal Virgins, who were the emblems of the state and the guarantees of its economic well-being.[14] Elagabalus's marriage to her was meant to flatter, not insult, the religion of Rome. The theory was that the great Syrian priest of Jupiter (Baal) was now united with the symbol of Roman divinity. As a deduction from this view, the statue of Caelestis (or Urania) was summoned from Carthage to be the bride of the Emesene Baal. The moon, that is to say, was married to the sun. But it was of no avail. The whole event did not make a good impression.

Things got even worse when Elagabalus fell out with Severus Alexander – who was at this stage quite popular, it seems, at Rome, notably with the praetorian guard. So Julia Maesa, deciding that the situation was hopeless, arranged on 11 or 13 March 222 to have Elagabalus killed by the soldiers, together with his mother Julia Soaemias. Severus Alexander (Plates 22–4) took his place, and became emperor for thirteen years, under the direction first of his grandmother Julia Maesa – who now said that he, not Elagabalus, was the (illegitimate) son of Caracalla – and then, for most of the time, under the guidance of his mother Julia Mamaea (Plates 25–6). He had been born in 207 or 208 in the Phoenician city of Arca (Caesarea ad Libanum; now Arqa), at the south-western foot of Mount Lebanon. His name, originally, had been Marcus Julius Gessius Alexianus. His father was Gessius Marcianus.

Like his cousin Elagabalus, Alexianus was priest of the Sun-god at Emesa, in spite of his youthful years. He took on the name Severus when he became emperor. It was to remind people of Caracalla, whose son, as he we saw, he claimed to be, that he changed his name Alexianus to Alexander – striving to imitate Alexander III the Great (Plate 13). Like Geta he included NOBILITAS among his coin-types, in order to stress the number of imperial generations that had allegedly preceded him. Another of Severus Alexander's coin-types was PERPETVITATI AVG., emphasizing the permanency of the imperial rule for which he stood.[15]

As for himself, he was simple, modest and chaste, but vacillating and ineffective, a 'silly boy' according to the later emperor Julian,[16] and completely tied to the apron-strings of his mother Julia Mamaea (Chapter 8; who gave him a wife, Orbiana, but then quarrelled with her). Severus Alexander was always unhappily conscious of his Syrian speech and manner. He did not like to be called a Syrian, and was insistent on his Roman descent and traditions.

Until his last years, when there was trouble on both the northern and eastern frontiers, the Roman world fortunately remained at peace, so the government was able to save money,[17] and introduce certain beneficial measures at home. For example, criminal law was made less harsh, the *collegia* at Rome were placed under official supervision, and measures of relief were introduced for land-owners.

But this policy of productive benevolence was magnified by historians into a fictitious senatorial recovery. Thus the *Historia Augusta* (see Appendix) pronounces, at great length, that Severus Alexander's reign had been a Golden Age of restored senatorial power and control – a sort of reversion to the time of Augustus. But all these elaborate insistences appear to be unfounded. The writer of the *Historia* has transformed the insignificant young man into an ideal monarch, furnished with an extensive collection of good qualities, and allegedly the promoter of salutary conservative changes, which were welcomed by the author (or his source). As for the revival of senatorial authority, it is plausible, at most, to accept the indication, confirmed from elsewhere, that Julia Maesa and Julia Mamaea, eager to create a reassuring impression after the disastrous ideas of Elagabalus, created a committee of sixteen members of the senate – possibly an offshoot of a bigger senatorial Council – to assist the young Severus Alexander during the years before he reached adulthood. But the additional remark of the *Historia*, to the effect that these measures revived the dignity of the senate rather than its supremacy, is very much to the point.

As the historian Dio Cassius (see Appendix) imagines that Augustus's counsellor Maecenas had observed, the senate was the recipient of sufficient deference if it was permitted the *appearance* of power – in other words, if it kept its prestige. Under Severus Alexander, even Elagabalus's principal adviser Comazon Eutychianus maintained his position – becoming prefect of the city for the third time. And the unstoppable tendency towards military autocracy continued on its way, without any noticeable lack of impetus. Severus Alexander no doubt did do *something* (quoting Augustus) to bolster up the senate's dignity, after the excesses of Elagabalus. But that had to be paid for by rigid economy at court (Chapter 7). And that meant that members of the imperial house were accused of meanness: especially Julia Mamaea, although the huge sums of money she amassed were said to be intended for the praetorians.

But not for the legionaries, although both she and her son tried to keep them in good temper by liberal donatives. Yet the blow that finally fell upon the emperor came from the northern armies, which felt that in the face of the now, at last, much augmented German menace (Chapter 5) the Syrian rulers were neglecting them and wanted to return to the east – and had, furthermore, humiliated Rome by buying peace from the Germans. So Severus Alexander (who was allegedly in favour of strong discipline) and his mother Julia Mamaea, both of whom had left Rome early in 234, were murdered by the legionaries up on the German frontier on 18 or 19 March of the following year, in favour of Maximinus I, 'the Thracian'.

The fact was that the entire period had witnessed an enormous increase in the power of the Roman army, which eclipsed the senate and the rest of the population (Chapter 6).

5

THE PROVINCES AND ITALY
The *Constitutio Antoniniana*

Septimius Severus's changes in the nature of the army, and his enhancement of its role (Chapter 6): inevitably at the expense of the senate, moved Rome some way towards democracy – since the army officers were often of lower social standing than before, and there was legal protection for the lower classes from which the military caste was drawn. And the army's rise also coincided with, and in part caused, an improvement in the status of the provinces (from which Septimius himself originated), until they were much closer to the status of Italy and Rome.

It was not that Rome was neglected. One only has to see the great Severan buildings in the capital (Chapter 11) to know that this was not so.[1] But Italy was not what it had been. The country was obliged to house part of the army,[2] and by this time provided scarcely one-third of the members of the senate.

It was Africa from which Septimius came (Plate 4), and obviously Africa, under his rule, was privileged[3] (he visited its shores in 203/4 with his family, and perhaps in 208 as well; cf. Chapter 1). Another recipient of privilege was Syria,[4] the homeland of Septimius's wife Julia Domna (Chapter 8), and the land which produced the emperors Elagabalus and Severus Alexander. Privileged, too, were the countries on the Danube frontier, notably Pannonia, where Septimius declared himself emperor, with the support of its army, which provided the most important of his legions.[5]

Furthermore, Septimius was a great expander of the empire – PROPAGATOR IMPERII, as his coins and medallions tell:[6] the greatest expander, it has been said, since Trajan (98–117), and the last. There was renewed talk of pushing forward the northern frontier.[7] Africa was again to the fore, since there were dramatic advances in Tripolitana, where the border tribes had been restless: a fort was constructed at Golas (Bu Njem), on the edge of the territory of the Garamantes.[8] And the frontier was moved forward in Mauretania (Caesariensis) as well. Syria, also, was once more prominent, and, while being divided into two provinces so that no governor should become too important, obtained an extension in size as far as the River Tigris. At the same time, too, as a result of the campaigns of Septimius, important work was done to create a new province of Mesopotamia as a bulwark of the enlarged empire. Dura-Europus and Palmyra (Tadmor) were fortified so that their garrisons could defend this new province.[9] And Egypt, to which Septimius went in 199, was extensively reorganized, notably by the creation, for the first time, of city councils.[10]

But it was not only the frontier provinces that benefited from the new spirit. Additional colonies were established. In the province of Asia alone we know of four appeals by Lydians to the emperors against what they considered, no doubt rightly, to be grievances. Moreover, the Celtic language, as well as Punic, came to be used in official documents.[11]

Septimius talked in world terms: of the *genus humanum* and the *orbis*. Whether or not he fully appreciated Roman institutions, and whether or not his spirit was, in fact, alien to that of Rome, certainly his understanding of the empire and its needs was wide.

In the east, this policy of expansion was made possible by Septimius's wars against the Parthians. They had tried to take advantage of his concentration on Clodius Albinus in the west, in order to assert themselves against the Romans. However, as soon as he could after his defeat of Albinus, Septimius moved against them, for the first of two wars. On the whole, he was successful – for instance, as was noted above, he created or re-created the province of Mesopotamia, and he captured Ctesiphon. But he twice failed to take Hatra (which, as we have seen, had supported Pescennius Niger), the first time in 198 and the next time in 199. This second attack, which lasted for twenty days, was called off when it looked like proving victorious. It was said that the emperor's wife Julia Domna was responsible for the move, since on eastern religious grounds she opposed the plundering of the Sun-god's shrine there. But it is also possible that Septimius felt that his soldiers, or he himself, had had enough of the hot climate. What he mainly achieved, however, was to weaken the Parthians permanently (a dubious achievement in the end, as we have seen, since they were succeeded by the Persians) –

although he himself was not immune from the influences of the Parthian court (Chapters 9, 12).

Septimius Severus spent the last years of his life in Britain and died in 211 at Eburacum (York). That province, like Syria, had been divided into two, probably in 197.[12] And there was a report that Septimius, who moved very far north, intended to conquer the whole island,[13] thus eliminating the need for the Walls of Hadrian (117–38) and Antoninus Pius (138–61), and reverting to the idea of the conquest of Britain in its entirety that had supposedly been mooted by Cnaeus Julius Agricola (AD 40–93). But since, in fact, Septimius did a lot of work on Hadrian's Wall in northern Britain – for which he was warmly praised[14] – it seems likely that if he ever intended to conquer the whole island, he abandoned the plan.

It is not quite clear why he went to Britain in the first place. Was the situation there serious enough for that? Things had been reasonably well sorted out some years earlier: though it is true that a governor of the province had said he needed a bigger army, or the presence of the emperor himself.[15] As for Septimius, he may have intended at first to annex the whole island, as we saw, but could have been deterred by the savagery of the northern tribes, and by his own poor health, so that he ended up by repairing Hadrian's Wall. Or perhaps he intended the campaign as an attempt to get his two sons away from Rome, and reconcile them with one another, and show them to the soldiers, securing the army's loyalty towards them (cf. Chapter 3). For he took both of them with him to Britain (to which he was also escorted by all or part of the praetorian guard, Chapter 2). Moreover, at the end of his reign he gave both Caracalla and Geta the title of Britannicus, as well as assuming it himself. Probably what he was aiming at, in particular, was a signal, decisive military victory. And that is, no doubt, what he claimed to have achieved. But after his death his two sons, intent on worsting one another, gave up the whole enterprise, abandoning, in the process, the new, unfinished Carpow fort on the Tava (Tay).[16] However, Caracalla's subsequent operations in Germany, whatever their immediate outcome, did at least postpone the threat from that quarter for twenty years.

His *Constitutio Antoniniana* (212) appears to us one of the outstanding features of the period, although whether it seemed the same to contemporaries is uncertain. Perhaps they just regarded it as a further stage in the tendencies already noted under Caracalla's father Septimius, to level citizens and other subjects.[17] At any rate that is what the *Constitutio* did, because its principal purpose was to make the vast majority of the free population of the empire into Roman citizens. The only exceptions were people called the *dediticii*, and there has been a great deal of discussion about who these were. It may be concluded, with some confidence, that they were tribesmen from beyond the Danube or Euphrates who had been recently conquered, had surrendered to the Romans, and had come into their empire lured by its higher living standards and better security.

Very probably one of Caracalla's motives in promulgating the *Constitutio Antoniniana* was to obtain increased revenue from the inheritance and manumission taxes that citizens paid.[18] But the enactment was also symbolic of a vast change that had gradually overtaken the Roman empire. It was now a *communis patria*, a common homeland and commonwealth, the ultimate unified development of autocratic power, in which provincials were as good as Italians and their equal partners, like all the inhabitants of Alexander III the Great's universal state. The *Constitutio* also universalized religion, and struck an impressively democratic note, somewhat diminished by the ever-increasing legal difference between higher and lower ranks of society, the *honestiores* and *humiliores*.[19]

Perhaps this democratic element was the fruitful result of giving jurists so much prominence on the imperial Council (Chapter 9). Alternatively, such men may have been disconcerted by a decision with so obviously political implications. In any case, however, now that jurists fulfilled such a large role, it is difficult to believe that none of them was concerned with the *Constitutio* at all.

But it was also a grandiose act calculated to distract attention from the emperor Caracalla's own family troubles, notably his murder of his brother Geta; while at the same time, as we saw, it raised more money, since now there were many more citizens to pay the manumission and bequest taxes required from men of that status (Chapter 7). On the debit side, the *Constitutio* made it harder to attract ambitious people into the army, seeing that all the soldiers, except those in native formations (*numeri*; Chapter 6) were now citizens, non-citizen auxiliaries having ceased to exist.

Caracalla, although militaristic, followed up a distressing massacre at Alexandria in 215 by forming the remarkable idea of marrying the daughter of Artabanus V, the king of Parthia (*c.* 213–224/6). Artabanus rejected the project, saying that she would not be happy married to a Roman. But his real reason was that he felt that the arrangement would subordinate him to Rome. Yet the idea, even if too much influenced by the utopian model of Alexander the Great,[20] had something to be said for it. Parthia was collapsing anyway, and this would at least have left it with an honourable status. As for the Romans, they would not have had to fight any more expensive, unsatisfactory eastern wars against their principal rivals, who the Parthians, as long as they lasted, were. As it was, Artabanus's refusal gave Caracalla an excuse to invade Parthia (by a trick) in 215, attempting for a short time to annex Armenia (although it had remained neutral, under the influence of subsidies). And his successor Macrinus, who restored that country to client status, got involved in a fresh invasion from Artabanus, from which he was accused of extricating himself dishonourably, by giving back to the Parthian king all their prisoners of war, together with a gift of 200 million *sestertii*; although it has also been argued that he did not act in any degrading fashion. In any case, he felt able, at least for a few months, to celebrate a Parthian victory, from 1 January 218, when the peace was sealed.

In 226 or 227 the Parthians, weakened by the attacks of Septimius, were superseded by the much more formidable Persians under Ardashir, against whom, following their invasion of Mesopotamia (230) and their preposterous claim that the River Strymon (Struma) in Europe was their true frontier (as it had been the frontier of their remote Persian ancestors), Severus Alexander was less than victorious. He launched an ambitious three-pronged invasion of their territory, in which his southern army met with disaster, whereas he himself, in command of the central force, never arrived on the scene at all. Perhaps the climate was partly to blame. And he himself suffered from dysentery.

But then, with the Persians fortunately inactive – for the invasion by Severus Alexander had at least so enfeebled them that they were unable to make any vigorous response – he felt obliged to leave the region altogether for the west. There the Alamanni beyond the River Rhenus (Rhine) – consisting of displaced tribal groups, which had quickly assimilated military techniques and had first made themselves known twenty years earlier (under Caracalla) – were now seriously threatening, having inflicted major destruction upon Roman centres, and destroyed many forts.

It is a curious lapse by Dio Cassius that he did not see this danger from the north, although he was well aware of the Persian menace in the east. But, in fact, Rome was now in a perilous pincer situation, facing grave and potentially fatal dangers in east and west alike.[21] The Romans had long paid subsidies to foreigners, and every emperor of this period had recourse to such measures, although they naturally gave rise to complaints at home – and they did not stave off invasions for ever.[22]

6

THE ARMY
The military monarchy

Augustus had established the number of Roman legions at twenty-eight, later diminished by losses to twenty-five. Trajan (98–117) disposed of thirty legions (rather larger in size), and Septimius thirty-three. He also increased the non-legionary soldiery (*numeri*), placing particular emphasis on mounted archers from Osrhoene and Palmyra, who were sent to all parts of the empire, however remote from the countries from which they came. Thus Septimius's army was considerably bigger than those of his predecessors. Its numbers, kept up by recruiting – which was now almost entirely conscript and compulsory – were calculated to ensure the defence of the empire and its emperor.

For Septimius, who tied the soldiers closely to his own imperial person, was well aware that everything depended on the army. And in consequence he drew the deduction that, if the soldiers were to be effective and loyal, they had to be better remunerated. As a result, not only were centurions now paid 8,333–33,333 *denarii* – instead of the 5,000–20,000 of the late first century AD – but legionaries received perhaps 500 *denarii* (or a little less?) instead of the 300 which had been their pay for the past century and more.

This was a much larger amount than soldiers had ever been given before. In consequence, from civilian quarters, there were complaints and lamentations about this 'bribery' of the army, which was interpreted as a cause of bad discipline; for which Septimius was blamed. Certainly, there were cases of indiscipline. But their attribution to the emperor did not take sufficient account of the inflation which had remorselessly diminished the purchasing power of the currency.

And indeed, because of this diminution, certain special measures had to be taken on behalf of the soldiers. Details will be given in the next chapter. But, for example, some of their bonuses were paid in gold,[1] which by-passed the debasement of the *denarius*. Most significant of all, however, was the fact that the soldiers now increasingly received payments in kind (forced out of civilians: cf. next chapter) as well as in cash. Moreover, it was apparently at this epoch that they were granted allowances to offset deductions from their pay for arms, clothing and rations (or at least such allowances, if granted earlier, were increased).

Legal recognition was also accorded to their unions with local women (who were often, nowadays, their compatriots). These concubines, that is to say, acquired an official status. And so did their sons, who often, in due course, followed their fathers into the army. As an encouragement to this hereditary self-sufficiency, garrisons were gradually assigned pieces of land, divided into allotments. That is to say, soldiers embarked upon farming, as well as upon other civilian activities such as trading, with special regard to the sale of stores and other products of the workshops they themselves had now created.[2]

As has been suggested above, the increased sums now paid to the soldiery owed a good deal to inflation. Nevertheless, when all their new or increased allowances were also taken into account, their terms under Septimius represented a genuine augmentation and improvement. Septimius gave them a number of additional privileges as well. For instance, we start hearing of clubs (*scholae*) for junior officers, providing not only social comforts and activities but also the sort of protective cover which an insurance society offers today. Furthermore, the tenure of military posts supplied stepping stones to a variety of civilian careers.[3] This soldiery was a novel élite, a caste which had very often risen from the ranks and endowed the empire with a great many of its most important officials – and indeed supplied a number of its emperors as well. And this new, and suitably grateful, aristocracy consisted to a large extent of frontier people. To a considerable extent, the civil service was militarized, as well as being strengthened by military detachments. Moreover, new veteran colonies were given a military character, and peasant communities were assimilated to army garrisons. Mention must also be made of Septimius's decision to post a new legion, II Parthica, inside Italy itself, at Albanum (Albano) on the bank of the Alban Lake. This meant that there was a large multiplication of troops on Italian soil. It was located there in order to protect the country from barbarian invasions and in order to overawe the senate. Moreover, this legion in Italy served as a sort of mobile field force.

But it was the troops on the Danube and in Germany, however little they were liked in Rome, which were the strongest,[4] and received the most favours (although their commanders were never, nowadays, their compatriots, so as to prevent military rebellions as much as possible; and for the same reason, from the time of Caracalla onwards, no frontier province contained more than two legions). Macrinus complained to the senate about Caracalla's pay increase to the legionaries (212) – comprising a rise, for the rank and file at least, of one-half – although he himself gave them a donative (as well as deifying Caracalla).

The various armies did not get on very well with one another, although the emperors tried to pretend that they did: hence the insistence on CONCORDIA MILITVM. *Numeri*, non-legionary troops – national units of semi-militarized peasants – were also increased in the place of 'auxiliaries' (Chapter 5). For example, eastern mounted archers probably reached their peak under Severus Alexander.

All this enlargement of the powers of the soldiery inevitably meant a diminution of the power of the senate. The speech of Maecenas in Augustan times, invented by Dio Cassius (Appendix), does not really signify that the senate's powers were restored in the historian's lifetime; it was, rather, a tribute to the prestige of that body, and a hope that this would be maintained or revived. The senate's powers had been damaged not only by the stationing of troops in Italy, but also by the executions of its members by Septimius Severus (which may well have mirrored a deliberate desire to abase the senate). And previously senatorial military commands were opened up to knights (equestrians) during the reign of Septimius.

In any case, most of the senators had increasingly become large provincial land-owners, of considerable social importance, it is true, but unconcerned with public service. The active senate was only a small core of the senatorial class, probably men mostly in their thirties or forties. But even they were virtually forced to ratify what the emperor or army had decided. And neither the emperor nor the army was very fond of them: Septimius's dying instructions to his sons to enrich the soldiers may well have been sound advice, however little the senators liked what he said. Indeed he virtually administered their death-blow. This was already clear enough when Septimius executed senators – and when he first told the army, not the senate, about the deification of Commodus, which he then left it to the senators to ratify. Macrinus and Elagabalus merely notified the senate of their accession, as was noted, and evoked criticism. Moreover, the civil service, as we have seen, was militarized. The emperor and his Council had become like a general and his staff.

Edward Gibbon had this to say about Septimius's relations with the army and senate:

Till the reign of Septimius, the virtue and even the good sense of the emperors had been distinguished by their zeal or affected reverence for the senate, and by a tender regard to the nice frame of civil policy instituted by Augustus.

But the youth of Severus had been trained in the implicit obedience of camps, and his riper years spent in the despotism of military command. His haughty and inflexible spirit could not discover, or would not acknowledge, the advantage of preserving an intermediate power, however imaginary, between the emperor and the army. He disdained to profess himself the servant of an assembly that detested his person and trembled at his frown. He issued his commands, where his request would have proved as effectual, assumed the conduct and style of a sovereign and a conqueror, and exercised, without disguise, the whole legislative as well as the executive power. The victory over the senate was easy and inglorious. Every eye and every passion was directed to the supreme magistrate . . .

In the reign of Septimius Severus, the senate was filled with polished and eloquent slaves from the eastern provinces, who justified personal flattery by speculative principles of servitude . . . and descanted on the inevitable mischiefs of freedom.[5]

Subsequently, too, the tendency continued. 'All the treasures are yours', the militaristic Caracalla said to his soldiers.[6] He habitually wore uniform (as his father, too, often had). And he gave the army huge gifts of money after Geta's death, as well as further increasing their pay – although they sometimes behaved badly and turbulently, alleging, for example, that the emperor preferred barbarians to them-selves[7] (and noting, no doubt, that barbarian imperial bodyguards had been revived).

Macrinus had trouble with the soldiers, complaining to the senate, as we saw, that they cost too much money. Elagabalus, liberal though he, too, felt he must be, had two men executed for tampering with the troops. And Severus Alexander did not underestimate their importance, as his mother's readiness to offer them donatives showed. But although he was, at first at least, quite popular with the army, a series of mutinies suggested that this situation did not last. And he was not very successful in the eastern field (Chapter 5) (though, if we look elsewhere, he sensibly built and restored Danubian as well as British roads).[8] Moreover, his attempts to reduce army costs was not liked by the soldiers, and his final failure to do what was expected of him on the northern frontier caused his and Julia Mamaea's deaths.

In other words, he had failed to control the army, which had come to realize that it was indispensable, and that it was top dog. How right it was, we may repeat, to call this whole period 'the military monarchy', and to observe that there had been a shift from the civilian to the military character of the Roman world. Moreover, the loyalty of the soldiers was now primarily directed towards whatever emperor they chose to favour, and not towards the state of Rome that those emperors professed to rule. The army (particularly in the Danubian region) had now become the masters of the empire, and determined the policies and despotisms of its rulers, from the time of Septimius and his son Caracalla onwards.

Septimius, as we saw, in order to purchase the soldiers' fidelity and prevent renewed civil wars, vastly improved their conditions, so much so that he was accused of weakening their discipline – and what he and his successors certainly did was to impose a heavy burden on the budget (Chapter 7). Despite liberal intentions by some rulers, imperial power – as against that of the senate and other leading Romans – was ever on the increase (financial need made it seem even more essential). And it was only the army that could enforce this power, and allow the emperors they selected to get on with the job.

7

FINANCE

Financiers, said C. J. Bullock,

> have always known that politics and finance are closely related, but they have sometimes appeared to differ in their statements concerning the nature of the relationship. . . .
>
> The whole truth was admirably put by James Wilson. . . . 'Finance is not mere arithmetic; finance is a great policy. Without sound finance, no government is possible; without sound government, no sound finance is possible.'[1]

This was very true of the Roman empire. By far the most serious problem that confronted the emperors concerned money. The entire history of the Roman empire could be rewritten in terms of finance, although this formidable question has not often been met: R. Duncan Jones has done something to fill the gap by his *Money and Government in the Roman Empire* (1994).

The financial difficulties that the Roman world faced under Septimius Severus were especially severe. It seems that there had been, and still was, a good deal of inflation, although our authorities do not tell us much about it. And Commodus – under whom a serious rise of prices certainly took place[2] – had left the treasury practically empty: a situation that was by no means helped by Didius Julianus's purchase of the emperorship, even though he failed to pay the price he had bid for it.

But what was really ruinous for the empire was the expensiveness of the army, which went up enormously. It must have cost a great deal of money for Septimius Severus to fight and win his civil wars, and then to conduct campaigns against the Parthians[3] and British, not to speak of the outlay on imperial defences in general. First of all, there was the question of military remuneration. Before

Septimius, the army had been poorly paid, particularly when one bears in mind what seems, as has been said, to have been a continual inflation. Yet now, with the soldiers so powerful, this changed. Admittedly Septimius did his best to keep matters within bounds. On his accession, for example, the soldiers demanded an enormous increase in pay, but he gave them much less than they asked for. Even that, however, added up to an augmentation by one-third, and was an extremely heavy financial burden. It was augmented to a very great extent not only by subsequent substantial pay increases, under Septimius and Caracalla (Chapter 6), but also by the donatives they felt it necessary to add. These were special money gifts (originally spoils, which were, incidentally, still obtained in the eastern wars) handed out by the emperors on their accessions or on other special occasions.

It had long been customary to supplement army pay by such bonuses. And after the transient predecessors of Septimius lost military support (and had been killed) – partly because they failed to hand over the donatives they had promised – there were sharp increases in the size and frequency of these awards, which Septimius and those after him felt to be necessary in order to keep themselves on the throne and alive. As was suggested in the last chapter, Septimius gave constant and extensive donatives, both to the praetorian guard and the legions – whose donatives are implied by the series of coins commemorating these units. Indeed, they were said to have been the largest donatives ever to have been given, and that is what they probably were. And they were supplemented, as we saw, by gifts in kind – in an empire which was insufficiently monetized – that is to say by levying supplies of foodstuffs and other goods (*annona militaris*), as a further inducement to maintain military support for the emperor.[4] This had been done before, particularly in national emergencies. Now, however, the practice was organized on a far more systematic scale.[5]

Once collected from civilians, the proceeds of these levies in kind were recycled to the troops in the form of free distributions of rations, clothing and the materials needed to make arms and equipment. It was also apparently from the time of Septimius that the men and women in each province were required to hand over food direct to the troops stationed within its borders. Land-owners extracted the required products from their tenants, and the leading officials of the cities were ordered to see that their populations contributed what was demanded. Worst of all, perhaps, was the unforseeable irregularity of such claims, which fell like thunderbolts upon the inhabitants. It may seem strange, at first sight, that so vast an empire could not maintain an army of between a quarter and half a million strong without these levies reminiscent of a prehistoric non-monetary economy. But food, clothing, weapons and armour were expensive to produce and export. The soldiers had to have them in great quantities. And they could only have them if the subjects of the empire contributed the materials.

So the army had become a huge burden on the state and public. And the equestrian procurators, too, whose numbers rose from 136 to 174, had to be paid. But under Septimius the public, too, were not neglected, especially at Rome itself. The *congiaria* to civilians there consisted of gigantic distributions, to over 100,000 people, of free grain and oil[6] and medicine, at festivals and on other festive occasions. For Septimius felt obliged to go in for this sort of thing on a vast and unprecedented scale, as well as giving costly Games. Like other emperors, that is to say, he felt that the civilian populace presented a threat, and needed to be kept quiet and happy. Yet these *liberalitates* imposed an additional severe strain on the treasury. Nevertheless, such lavish imperial giving was required as part of the Golden Age which was allegedly coming into existence.[7]

Although, however, Dio Cassius blamed Septimius for this expenditure, and although the emperor had to spend, or did spend, such a gigantic amount on the army and the civilian population, the astonishing thing is that having at first found the imperial coffers empty he left them full at his death.

How did he raise so much money? He did so by various means, and took a great deal of trouble to achieve this. First, there was wealth taken over from the Parthians. And, secondly, there was probably heavier taxation: the land-tax and tributary poll-tax, the direct contributions which non-citizens normally had to pay, were one way, for the time being, of raising revenue.[8] Another way was by the steady transfer of funds from the wealthy classes to loyal soldiers, which we hear little about but must have existed: local liturgies (*munera*) clearly cost the richer people a lot. Furthermore, Septimius confiscated a great deal of money from Plautianus (and his followers) and, earlier – apparently on an unparalleled scale – from the prosperous men who had supported his rivals. Or he took over their estates and sold them, after their previous owners had been executed.[9]

He also maintained stricter control over *collegia* (guilds). And he followed earlier precedents by debasing the coinage, in order to give himself the quantities of money that he required. Didius Julianus had sharply reduced the weight of the *aureus* and *denarius*. Septimius left the *aureus* unchanged, but reduced the silver content of the *denarius* to 50 per cent – so that the ratio between gold and silver deteriorated, and Severan *denarii* were probably discounted in commerce.[10] His Parthian expeditions, too, brought in much gold as loot (although, as Dio Cassius said, these campaigns also cost a lot). So by such means Septimius raised enough money to meet his vast expenses. Yet it was still something of a miracle that he did so, and that (after taking a very large sum of money with him to Britain) he left the treasury full of funds when he died (even though we do not know for certain how much he left).

Caracalla proved unable to keep this up. He told the soldiers that all the money he had was theirs, and he meant it. For in addition to the vast expenses of his eastern campaigns, he gave them enormous gifts, in the form of increases of pay (by one-half), donatives, ration allowances and discharge grants. His donatives were particularly large just after the murder of Geta, when the praetorians, especially, needed to be assuaged; and there was also a *congiarium* in 214, in honour of Caracalla's Triumph. He also built costly buildings (Chapter 11) and paid out substantial subsidies to Rome's enemies, subsidies which were, in fact, cheaper than fighting, but were criticized all the same, ostensibly because they were humiliating, but also because they cost a lot of money (see also below).

However, Caracalla had various ways of raising funds, in order to compensate for these expenses. First of all, he doubled the 5 per cent taxes on manumissions and bequests and introduced new taxation; and the *Constitutio Antoniniana*, conferring widespread citizenship (Chapter 5), meant that more people paid manumission and bequest taxes. Moreover, he demanded an extraordinary income tax known as the *aurum coronarium*, crown money, originating from a Republican custom of levying gold crowns for Triumphs, although now the crowns were commuted into cash.

But above all Caracalla embarked on a new and drastic means of debasing the coinage. This he did, not only by reducing the weight of the *aureus* by 10 per cent, but by issuing, in the usual poor-quality silver, a double *denarius* piece, which we know as the *antoninianus*:[11] its advantage to Caracalla being that it weighed a great deal less than two *denarii*, a point which people were encouraged to forget because of the coin's fine appearance, which gave an artificial impression of imperial munificence and prosperity. Emperors at this period portrayed (Juno) Moneta, Money, on the coinage, and displayed the Tres Monetae as well – a term of which the exact meaning is uncertain, but it is clear that Moneta was linked with Aequitas (which also appears),[12] representing authoritative fair dealing, care for accurate and honest measures and weights. But this was made a mockery of by the bare-faced expedient of the *antoninianus*. However, the coin kept Caracalla above water.[13] And, in spite of his high expenses, he left quite a lot of money in the treasury.

But Macrinus squandered all or most of it, although his lavish gifts to soldiers and civilian public alike did not serve to give him adequate support, especially as his donations to the army were accompanied by a diminution of pay for new recruits, and by complaints about his subsidies to foreigners (for which he also blamed Caracalla; Chapter 5). Moreover, he increased taxes – with the result that there was an outcry demanding that gold and silver statues should be melted down – and his presents to civilians, as we saw, concentrated on grain, not money.[14] Elagabalus also bestowed liberalities and donatives, wastefully it was said – there were no fewer than four *congiaria* during the four years of his reign – and continued to offer the type of Moneta on his medallions, though he went on issuing the *antoninianus*.

But when Severus Alexander, after a *congiarium* on his accession, subsequently proclaimed himself RESTITVTOR MONETAE,[15] it may have been (despite various other modern interpretations) because he had ceased to coin *antoniniani* at all, and wanted to get the credit for abandoning such a dishonest endeavour to make money: AEQVITAS may now signify this abandonment (although the weight of the *aureus* was again diminished). And the same emperor, to the indignation of many Romans, offered German delegates a good deal of money, which they accepted.

Defence did, however, become a severe financial strain, and Severus Alexander realized the dangers of excessive expenditure. In consequence, while trying to keep the troops in good temper by liberal donatives (accompanied by judicious generosities to civilians), he tried to diminish army costs, while also, as was mentioned elsewhere, exercising rigorous economies at court – including the sale of the palace dwarfs – since he was well aware that people were complaining about the cost of living.[16] Yet all this signified that he was regarded as mean (except by the land-owners, whom he helped:

perhaps by remitting part of the *aurum coronarium*). And that particularly applied to his mother Julia Mamaea (under whose thumb he wholly remained) – however much she might say that the money she had amassed was intended for the guard (Chapter 2). This alleged stinginess was one of the reasons why he and she were both murdered, in 235.

8

THE SYRIAN WOMEN

One of the outstanding aspects of the period, and one that is of particular interest today, is the unusual prominence of powerful women. We are used to hearing about Messalina and Agrippina the younger in the first century, because we have a great historian (Tacitus) who writes about them. But we hear much less about the cunning and ambitious Severan women, Julia Domna and her sister Julia Maesa, and the latter's daughters Julia Soaemias and Julia Mamaea (Plates 5, 6, 7, 21, 25, 26), because there is no first-class historian who writes about these startling 'Syrian princesses', as Gibbon called them.[1] Yet, certainly, those women for a time were in supreme control of the huge Roman empire.

It is perhaps paradoxical that the most able of all these women, Julia Domna, possessed, at least at first, less supreme power than the others. That is because she had a husband, Septimius Severus, who was himself extremely dominant. He had been married before, to Paccia Marciana, to whom there was a memorial at Cirta (Constantine). In 193 he gave his two daughters by her in marriage. But he did not, apparently, mention the name of Paccia Marciana in his autobiography.

When, however, he went to Syria in 179 to command a legion (IV Scythica) he had been much impressed by Julia Domna, then a girl of 10. Dio's story that she was of low birth was wrong: she was a daughter of the hereditary high priest of Baal at Emesa (Homs) (Julius Bassianus). But what really impressed Septimius, superstitious as he must have been, was her royal horoscope. Later on, partly because of this, he summoned her to him, to be his wife.

She was certainly a decisive woman. It was she, people said, who urged the crushing of Pescennius Niger and Clodius Albinus, even if the youthful age of her children prevented her from being in

Septimius's company at that time – although she was said to have insisted on the promotion of Caracalla (who was probably her son; cf. next chapter). And later she joined Septimius in the Parthian wars, allegedly intervening, as has been said, to prevent the sacking of a temple at Hatra. Indeed she may well have influenced Septimius in other matters of religion as well. She had a reputation for promiscuity and incest, perhaps spread (falsely?) by Plautianus (Chapter 2), with whom she had a serious row.

She was also a cultured person, who was allegedly 'a devoted admirer of all rhetorical exercises', and was supposed to have maintained a kind of salon,[2] of which Philostratus (Chapters 10, 12) and the Thessalian sophist Philiscus (who held the Chair of Rhetoric at Athens) are the only known representatives; Philostratus described her as 'philosophical'. But above all, despite her quarrel with Plautianus, she participated fully in her husband's official activities (and surely did not conspire against him), so that she was an empress in a new sense of the term, and was honoured as such, and as a goddess.[3] There are impressive busts, coins and medallions and inscriptions honouring her. And the best-preserved relief on the Arch of the Argentarii (Bankers) at Rome (Chapter 11) shows her sacrificing with Septimius. She wears a Syrian veil and diadem, and raises her hand, palm outwards, in an oriental gesture of adulation. The Arch at Lepcis Magna (Chapter 11) shows sacrifices in her honour. Yet she remained subordinate to her husband.

When Septimius died, however, Julia Domna, whose coins had already stressed her FECVNDITAS, had a great deal to say. She employed titles usually reserved for the emperor. It was also asserted that she was against the geographical division of the empire between Caracalla and his brother Geta – although developments in the distant future showed that such a plan was by no means impracticable – and that Geta was murdered in her arms, by Caracalla's agents (Chapter 4). Nevertheless, she continued to work hard on behalf of Caracalla – who apparently trusted her, perhaps in a warped sort of way. At any rate, he allowed, or encouraged, her to bear the titles *pia felix, mater Augusti, mater senatus, mater castrorum* and *mater patriae*. While he himself spent most of the subsequent years with his army in the east, it was she who presided over the administration in Rome, thus finding an expression for her political talents (despite the hostility a woman in such a position inevitably encountered). According to one view, she was partly or largely responsible for the perhaps to some extent idealistic, or at least not narrowly Roman, *Constitutio*

Antoniniana (Chapter 4). On hearing, with horror, of the assassination of Caracalla (217), although carefully treated by his murderer and successor Macrinus, she died (of cancer) or committed suicide at Antioch. She was in her mid-forties. Elagabalus or Severus Alexander deified her.

Her sister was the somewhat less cultured but scarcely less able Julia Maesa, whose formidable features are well displayed on coins (Plate 21). She had been the wife of Julius Avitus, a Syrian of consular rank. After the death of Caracalla she was misguidedly ordered by Macrinus to return, with her two daughters (Julia Soaemias and Julia Avita Mamaea), and their sons Elagabalus and Alexianus, to Emesa, where her vast wealth powerfully influenced the Roman soldiery in Syria.[4] Thus she presided over the victorious battle in which Gannys, supposedly the lover of her daughter Julia Soaemias,[5] defeated the forces of Macrinus; so that her 14-year-old son Elagabalus – who was said to have distinguished himself in the engagement – became emperor. But Julia Maesa (who, despite the emphasis on chastity, *pudicitia*, on the coins issued in her honour, declared that Elagabalus was the son of Caracalla) was the true ruler. She even, apparently, attended the senate. After all events, she was astutely advised.

As time went on, however, Julia Maesa realized that Elagabalus, very young and inadequately controlled by his mother (her daughter) Julia Soaemias, was too eccentric to rule the empire. So she persuaded him to 'adopt' his cousin Alexianus (the son of Maesa's other daughter Julia Mamaea), allegedly so that Alexianus should perform the official administrative tasks and Elagabalus – whose lack of interest in public affairs was conspicuous and shocking – could concentrate on his priestly duties (Chapter 12). But when this did not work (partly because the two youths did not get on with one another), she had Elagabalus murdered, along with his mother – one of her own daughters – so that Alexianus could become emperor instead, under the name of Severus Alexander. And Julia Maesa now pronounced that he, not Elagabalus, was the son of Caracalla. But Julia Maesa died not very long afterwards, at a date that is not certain, and was deified.

It was now that female rule really came into its own, since when Severus Alexander came to the throne he was (like Elagabalus before him) only 14, so that his mother Julia Mamaea, who was the second daughter of Julia Maesa (and wife of a Syrian from the cult centre

Arca Caesarea ad Libanum, Arqa), and had possibly connived in the death of Elagabalus, inevitably and necessarily had to look after the boy – and thus ruled the vast empire.[6]

Moreover, when Alexander grew up, although he was quite popular, at first, with the troops, he remained vacillating and ineffective, so that Mamaea continued to rule. He was often known, merely, as the 'son of Mamaea', whereas she was described as 'Mother of the Augustus', as well as 'Mother of the Camp'.[7] This was the climactic point of feminine power. And yet, owing to the dearth of good historians of the period (and the feeble fictitiousness of the *Historia Augusta*'s life of her son; cf. Appendix), not very much is known about her, or her obvious qualities, except from the self-praise of the abundant coins and medallions issued in her honour. A medallion equates her with Victory and Ceres.[8] Ulpian, at this time, conceded that an Augusta could be given an emperor's privileges (Chapter 9). Although it fell to her, among much else, to choose the members of Severus Alexander's Council, she usually exercised her power with unobtrusive prudence, apparently cultivating good relations not only with the Christians (Hippolytus and Origen, Chapter 12), but also with the senate; yet she did manage to quarrel with the wife she had given her son, Sallustia Barbia Orbiana, the daughter of Seius (?) Sallustius Macrinus (who, some said, wrongly, was made Caesar).

Julia Mamaea also made the mistake, as we have seen (Chapter 2), of amassing too much personal wealth. Her excuse that it was intended for the praetorians fell on deaf ears. She gained a reputation for meanness, which, together with the military weakness of herself and her son – whom she accompanied to the north, where they were said to have made a disgraceful peace with the Germans (Chapter 5) – eventually alienated the army and led to the murder of both of them in 235. Julia Mamaea was in her early forties.

The extraordinary period in which women ran the Roman empire was at an end. And, it may be repeated, we know too little about it, because there is no ancient historian who gives us sufficient, or sufficiently reliable, information.

Plate 1 Pertinax. *Dupondius* (British Museum)*

This is a coin of Pertinax, who reigned very briefly in 193, and failed to replace the excesses of his predecessor Commodus by a régime of austerity. (But Septimius Severus, when he came to the throne in the same year, started his reign by posing as the heir and avenger of Pertinax, whom he deified and whose name he adopted.) The radiate crown on the coin indicates that it is a *dupondius* and not one of the *asses*, on which this sort of crown does not appear.

Plate 2 Didius Julianus. *Sestertius*, issued during his brief reign (193)
(British Museum)

After becoming emperor by disgracefully purchasing the throne at an auction after the murder of Pertinax, he proved unable to confront Septimius Severus, who came down from the Danube with the legions stationed in that area. Didius Julianus was killed, and Septimius took his place.

*The gold denomination is the *aureus*, the silver (or, by the time of Septimius Severus, base silver or billon) denominations are the *antoninianus* (introduced by Caracalla and temporarily suspended by Severus Alexander), *denarius*, and (occasionally) *quinarius*, and the bronze denominations are the *sestertius, dupondius, as* and (rarely) *semis*. Originally the *sestertius* and *dupondius* had been made of brass, i.e. copper mixed with zinc (*orichalcum*), and the *as* and *semis* of copper. But by now the purity and distinctness of these metals had been eroded, and all were more or less of bronze, in which the zinc of the brass and red purity of the copper were replaced by tin and/or lead alloys (M. Grant, *Roman Imperial Money* (London, 1954), pp. 240f.). The bronze provincial and local coinages of the east had denominations of their own, mainly Greek.

Plate 3 Septimius Severus. Antike Sammlungen, Glyptothek, Munich (Alinari)
The busts of Septimius Severus, which are fairly numerous, combine a back-
ward-looking, Antonine appearance with certain features that betoken the
future: in fact, they stand for the new Severan epoch. The general impression
is Antonine – we are expected to see Septimius as the rightful heir and successor
of Antoninus Pius and Marcus Aurelius, to whose family he, fictitiously, claimed
to belong. Yet the hair-style is more akin to modern times, with echoes of the
Egyptian god Serapis. Nevertheless, if Septimius possessed any markedly un-
Roman features, they are not made apparent on these busts.

Plate 4 Bronze *sestertius* of Septimius Severus. M. Grant, *The World of Rome*
(1960), plate 9 (British Museum)

Septimius assumes the name of Pertinax, whose memory he honoured, and is
IMPERATOR for the fourth time (194–5) (L. SEPT. SEV. PERT. AVG. IMP IIII). He
also wears military uniform, a fitting tribute to his own military success in
putting down Pescennius Niger (as he later defeated Clodius Albinus). (And on
the reverse appears AFRICA, which was his homeland, since he came from Lepcis
Magna in Tripolitana. Septimius enriched Africa (not least his home town) with
many buildings, and here he celebrates his country, which is personified wearing
an elephant-skin head-dress, and apparently holding ears of corn in a fold of
her robe. At her feet, partly seen, is a lion. On other coins Septimius honours
the gods who received special veneration in Africa and his own family, Hercules
and Bacchus.)

Plate 5 Bust of Julia Domna (Alinari)

Julia Domna was the second wife of Septimius Severus. She was a Syrian by birth. According to some reports, she gathered round herself a collection of learned men. She was eclipsed from *c.* AD 200 to 205 by the praetorian prefect Plautianus, but regained influence after his fall. After the death of her husband, she attempted to reconcile his sons Caracalla and Geta, but without success. Nevertheless, she was extremely powerful and active at Rome while Caracalla was in the east. On hearing of his death in 217, she died or committed suicide.

Plate 6 Coin of Septimius Severus and Julia Domna. *Aureus.* Sale catalogue
(AD 200–1) (Private, Michael Grant)

Julia Domna, a Syrian, was a new type of empress: not only did she get on well,
apparently, with her husband (although they must have had some differences of
opinion about his powerful praetorian prefect, Plautianus, whose relations with
her were very bad indeed), and fully shared his imperial tasks and responsibilities,
but she was extremely cultured: though whether she actually maintained a
literary salon, as was asserted, is doubtful. But it is justified to see in her the
founder and prime begetter of the series of Syrian women who played such a
vast part in the conduct of the empire during the decades that followed. As for
Septimius Severus, he describes himself as PARTHICVS MAXIMVS to celebrate his
victories against the Parthians, although, as his two failures to capture Hatra
showed, they were incomplete: but they were sufficient to keep the Parthians
quiet and relatively shattered, with disastrous results for the Romans later on,
when the Parthians were superseded by the much more formidable Persians.

Plate 7 Septimius Severus, Julia Domna, Caracalla and Geta. *Aureus.* AD 202
(British Museum)

This gold coin compendiously illustrates both the importance of Septimius's
Syrian empress Julia Domna, whose portrait appears (frontally), and the insistence with which he pushed forward his sons Caracalla and Geta. The inscription
FELICITAS SAECVLI anticipates Septimius's celebration of the Secular Games in
204.

Plate 8 Geta(?). Museo Nazionale (Terme), Rome (Alinari)

The father of Caracalla and Geta, Septimius Severus, although (we are told) aware, at least at the end of his life, of the faults of Caracalla, persisted in the idea that after his death the empire could be shared between the two brothers: a duality of which his wife Julia Domna strongly disapproved. The present bust is usually identified with Geta, in all probability rightly (though it might represent his brother Caracalla). It depicts the prince as a boy. Septimius was always determined, from the earliest youth of his two sons, that they should jointly succeed him, although he promoted Geta rather late, possibly because Caracalla had taken such a dislike to his brother. Indeed, Septimius had not been dead for very long before Geta was murdered by Caracalla.

As for the character of Geta, we have various accounts, some good, some bad. The latter are no doubt amplified by the fact that he was the loser, and did not therefore control what was subsequently said.

Plate 9 Geta. Bronze *sestertius*. AD 203–8. Sale catalogue (British Museum)
Septimius Severus utilized the massive Secular Games and celebrations to public-
ize not only his elder son Caracalla but his younger son Geta, who is shown
here as CAESAR. Other coins of the same date honour him as consul, *pontifex*
and *princeps iuventutis*, although it took a long time before he joined his elder
brother as Augustus. On the reverse is a sacrificial scene, inscribed SAECVLARIA
SACRA. Since the central, sacrificing figure wears a beard, it is presumably
Septimius Severus himself, flanked by his sons. On the left is a man (or woman)
playing a flute, on the right another playing a harp. The reclining figure of the
Tiber is also to be seen. Behind is a temple, which has been identified by
Mattingly and Sydenham with the temple of Terra Mater, which, in the ritual
of Augustus, took place on the third night. This intrusion of personal religious
associations into a time-honoured state liturgy speaks volumes for the whole
policy of Septimius Severus.

Plate 10 Pescennius Niger. *Denarius* (British Museum)
Septimius Severus's claim to the imperial throne was quickly, but in the end
unsuccessfully, contested by Pescennius Niger in the east. His coin shows two
capricorns with a round shield, bearing a globe showing seven stars. The
inscription is IVSTI AVG., showing Pescennius's emphasis on this quality.

Plate 11 Clodius Albinus. *Aureus.* AD 193–7 (British Museum)
This is a coin bearing the head of Clodius Albinus (including the name of
Septimius, which may have formed part of his nomenclature), during the early
years of Septimius Severus's reign when he proclaimed Albinus to be his Caesar
and implied successor, instead of his own son Caracalla – a situation which was
abruptly reversed after Septimius had defeated and killed Pescennius Niger in
the east.

The reverse inscription is SAECVLO FRVGIFERO, that is to say, Clodius Albinus
proclaims a new era of abundance and prosperity. The god of this prosperity,
the *deus frugifer (Aion Karpophoros)*, is shown, holding corn-ears, between two
sphinxes. This indicates that he is to be identified with the Egyptian god Osiris.
At one time the coin-type was related to a divine patron of Hadrumetum in
north Africa, when Clodius Albinus was believed to have come from there: but
now that origin is doubted.

Plate 12 Caracalla. Museo Archeologico Nazionale, Naples (Alinari)

One of the turning-points in the history of Roman sculpture and art is repre-sented by these superb busts of the emperor Caracalla. They show a new brutality, ferocity and violence. One must assume that they had the approval of the emperor himself, who is similarly depicted on his coinage. This new quality is partly an echo of his own savage personality, which is thus stamped on his portrait-busts in no uncertain fashion, establishing a marked difference from the tranquil personalities which Antoninus Pius and Marcus Aurelius had wanted to display in their portraits.

It is not, perhaps, mistaken to see in these heads of Caracalla an echo of Alexander the Great, whom he so conspicuously admired and sought, and claimed, to imitate. But this new type of head is also symbolical of the new and tougher epoch in which Caracalla lived and reigned, an epoch in which the army, with which the emperor so wholeheartedly associated himself, was the ruler of the empire.

Caracalla's short, curly hair is a transition between the flowing, Hellenic or Hellenistic locks of his Antonine predecessors and the close-cropped heads of later rulers, such as Severus Alexander.

Plate 13 Gold medallion in memory of Alexander III the Great. Found at Abukir in Egypt. National Coin Collection, Berlin (M. Grant, *The Climax of Rome*, plate 39)

As a prominent feature of the fashionable cult of past heroes, there was an immense respect for Alexander III the Great (356–323 BC), especially in his native Macedonia, where this gold medallion was a prize at the Games of AD 242–3. The lasting reverence for Alexander was enhanced by Caracalla (his portrait appears on the other side of the medallion), who was particularly attached to his memory, and by Severus Alexander (it was in his reign that the medallion was created), who on coming to the throne changed his name from Alexianus to Alexander.

On this medallion Alexander the Great looks upwards, with the gaze into the heavens that had become so familiar in the third century, which was so devoted to the cult of the Sun and to monotheism.

Plate 14 Macrinus. Capitoline Museum, Rome (Alinari)

Macrinus emerged as emperor for one year (217–18). He had been quite a
good lawyer. However, as became rapidly evident, he did not – despite his
dynastic ambitions – command enough admiration or support to remain on the
imperial summit for long. Meanwhile his sculptors, like his moneyers, had to
endow him with all the grandeur and dignity that they could, and this is one
of the more impressive results of their efforts.

Plate 15 Coin of Diadumenian (Private, Michael Grant)

Diadumenian was the son and heir of Macrinus (217–18), whom he elevated first to the rank of Caesar and then to that of Augustus, in the forlorn hope of founding a dynasty. With the same hope, he gave him the traditional title of 'Prince of the Youth', and it is in this guise that the reverse shows him, with military standards.

Plate 16 Elagabalus. Capitoline Museum, Rome (Alinari)
It is hard to pin down for certain any authentic portrait-busts of Elagabalus, but this does appear to be one of them.

The shortage of such readily identifiable busts is surprising in one respect, but not in others. It is surprising because a great many of his coins have survived, presenting his portraits. It is unsurprising, first, because he was so young (14 to 18) that many might have thought that his appearance scarcely mattered, and secondly, because his reputation, after his death, fell into disrepute, so that a great many of his busts were destroyed or hidden away.

It would not, however, probably be a mistake to suppose that the sculptors of the time were encouraged to get away from the brutalism of Caracalla, and that this tendency extended to the portraiture of Elagabalus (although his women claimed that he was Caracalla's son: cf. caption to Plate 17).

Plate 17 Elagabalus. *Aureus* (British Museum)

Elagabalus so greatly rejoiced in his position as high priest of the God of the Sun (El-Gabal) at Emesa (Homs) in Syria that he even allowed specific mention of the deity to appear in the usually traditionalistic medium of the coinage. The present *aureus* was issued at Nicomedia (Izmit) in Bithynia, north-western Asia Minor, where his first winter as emperor was passed (218–19). The reverse bears the inscription SANCT[o] DEO SOLI ELAGABAL[o], accompanying a quadriga which contains the sacred conical black stone of Emesa, engraved with the sculpture of an eagle and surmounted by four parasols.

But on the obverse the emperor is called Marcus Aurelius Antoninus, which was his official name as the alleged son of Caracalla, whose father Septimius had, equally falsely, declared his adoption into the Antonine House.

Plate 18 Elagabalus: *Aureus*. Sale catalogue (British Museum)

We rely very much on the coins to show what Elagabalus really looked like. He is given the nomenclature 'Antoninus Pius Aug[ustus]' as an alleged, fictitious, descendant of the great Antonine House. The reverse shows him riding into Rome (ADVENTVS AVGVSTI.) where he had informed the senate of his accession – at the hands of the army – instead of seeking its permission to ascend the throne.

Plate 19 Julia Paula. *Denarius* (British Museum)

When Julia Maesa found the eccentricities of her grandson the emperor Elagabalus intolerable – or realized that they were creating a bad impression – she arranged for him to have a wife: or, rather, three successive wives, although some credit him with more. The first, Julia Paula, is portrayed here. But she did not last for long.

Plate 20 Aquilia Severa. *Sestertius* (British Museum)

This was the second of the (at least) three wives whom Julia Maesa induced her grandson the emperor Elagabalus to marry. Aquilia Severa was, however, a Vestal Virgin. And if this was intended as a compliment to Roman religion – marrying it, as it were, to the Syrian faith of the emperor – it misfired, since many leading Romans were shocked. Nevertheless, Elagabalus, after quickly discarding Aquilia Severa, then married her again, after he had ceased to be impressed by her successor Annia Faustina.

Plate 21 Julia Maesa, during the reign of her grandson Elagabalus (218–22)
(British Museum; M. Grant, *Roman Imperial Money* (1954), plate 40, no. 1)
Julia Maesa, although we do not hear of her from any first-class historian, was
the most powerful woman Rome had ever known, or would ever know. A
Syrian from Emesa (Homs), she was the grandmother of the eccentric young
emperor Elagabalus – and after she abandoned him was grandmother of the
next juvenile emperor as well, Severus Alexander, until she herself died not
long after his accession.

The reverse of this coin bears the type of PVDICITIA, female modesty and
chastity. Whether this was, in fact, one of Julia Maesa's characteristics we do
not know. But we do know that she proclaimed that both her daughters had
committed adultery with Caracalla, producing Elagabalus and Severus Alexander
respectively (cf. earlier captions).

Plate 22 Severus Alexander. Louvre, Paris (Alinari)
Severus Alexander was an inoffensive young man. But his sculptor here has
caught the spirit of the military monarchy, facing serious barbarian offensives,
by depicting him with the close-cropped hair of an army general.

Plate 23 Severus Alexander. Museo Archeologico Nazionale, Naples (Alinari)
There is something slightly ludicrous about the Roman taste for depicting
emperors as legendary heroes or ancient Greek figures. And this ludicrousness
becomes particularly apparent when we see here, for example, the unimpressive
Severus Alexander shown like the athletic and semi-divine Doryphorus of
Polyclitus.

Plate 24 Severus Alexander. *Sestertius.* Sale Catalogue (British Museum)
The reverse inscription of this coin, RESTITVTOR MON[*etae*], remains a mystery.
In what respect did Severus Alexander 'restore' the mint, or the Temple of
(Juno) Moneta, or the coinage? The problem is discussed in the text.
   On this obverse, the emperor is shown in military guise.

Plate 25 Julia Mamaea. Museo Nazionale (Terme), Rome (Alinari)

Portraits of Julia Mamaea, not always readily identifiable – although she had, to judge from her coins, a rather distinctive hair-style – recall a remarkable period in the history of the Roman empire, during which the supreme power was in the hands of a woman.

It was when 'the Syrian princesses' arrived on the scene, under the Severans, that this feminine rulership became truly established. And this was never more the case than during the reign of Severus Alexander. The emperor himself was at first only a boy, who needed his mother's control and decisiveness – his mother being Julia Mamaea. And he grew up to be a diffident and ineffective young man who was never able (and we do not know whether, except perhaps at the last moment, he even tried) to liberate himself from maternal direction and decision-making.

Plate 26 Julia Mamaea. Billon medallion (British Museum)

Julia Mamaea, the mother of the emperor Severus Alexander, is here given every possible honour, as befitted the ruler of the Roman empire, which she was and Severus Alexander was not.

(Her bust shows her wearing a crown ornamented with necklace and ears of corn. On her right arm she holds a *cornucopia*, and in her left hand there is a torch from which ears of corn are spreading. That is to say, she is identified with the goddess of plenty, Ceres (Demeter).)

The reverse bears the inscription FELICITAS PERPETVA. Julia Mamaea, seated, holds a sceptre. She is accompanied by three women, one of whom presents a globe to her, and another, Felicitas, holds a *caduceus*, the herald's staff of Mercury, as messenger of the gods, and emblem of trade and peace (the temple of Concord was adorned with a bronze *caduceus*).

On other pieces Mamaea is hailed as 'Mother of the Augustus' and 'Mother of the Camp' (MATER AVGVSTI ET CASTRORVM)

Plate 27 The Arch of Septimius Severus in the Forum (Anderson)

Triumphal Arches, with all their implications and demonstrations of grandeur, form an essential and prominent part of the monumental survival of ancient Rome – as of many of its provinces.

We can now see the Arch of Septimius Severus better than ever before, since the plastic cover which until recently muffled it up has been removed. It is a fitting monument to one of Rome's most able emperors, concentrating particularly, not least in the inscription which is to be seen on either side, upon his military achievements in the east. The Arch is also covered with reliefs, including, especially, massive panels telling the official version of the story of these campaigns. They are poorly preserved. But they include an imperial *adlocutio* (harangue) (right), women on the walls of a besieged city (centre), and Roman soldiers beside the bank of a river (left); and, below, a cavalry battle (right), the siege of an enemy city (centre) and enemy cavalry in flight (left). Unlike the design of the Arch itself, which conforms with tradition, the reliefs display a thoroughgoing abandonment of the traditional formulae of classical Greco-Roman art in favour of the styles of late antiquity.

Plate 28 Relief from the Arch of Septimius Severus, Lepcis Magna (Alinari)
The detail shown is from one of the four long exterior friezes. Two of them
described the Triumph, and two the unity of the imperial family, as well as the
divine protection they enjoyed.

In this chariot panel, a system of vertical accents emerges. The frontal display
of the figures on the chariot – for the emperor in his chariot, and his attendants,
confront the spectator – and the flattened horses, and the closed frontal phalanx
of spectators in military dress above the horses, and the 'zoning' of men in two
tiers – all these are early signs of the transformation from classical to the 'late
antique' abstract style.

> Standing in the center, the emperor steers the team, his head crowned with
> laurel, ribbons streaming behind. Triumphantly his sons push against their
> father, Caracalla on the right. Geta on the left. . . . Geta's face is chopped
> off. His memory was officially condemned after Caracalla had murdered
> him.
>   The chariot is shown in a peculiar view, part profile and part head-
> on. . . . The artist has subtly shifted the traditional imagery. The triumphant
> emperor no longer goes to Rome and Jupiter on the Capitol. He is at
> once the general and Jupiter, and presumably the procession shown took
> place in Lepcis itself.
>   (G. M. A Hanfmann, *Roman Art* (New York, 1975), p. 117

So here is a build-up of the central, imperial personage. This, one may say –
like the frontality that has already been mentioned – is a sign of the extent to
which, as the 'late antique' style develops, eastern motifs and manners have
begun to invade the western tradition.

Plate 29 The Sanctuary of Heliopolis (Baalbek) in Syria: reconstruction (Alinari)

The Sanctuary of Jupiter Heliopolitanus at Heliopolis (Baalbek) in Syria was one of the greatest and most complex shrines in the world, constructed over many Roman epochs.

It is by no means surprising that much building was done there during the Severan period, seeing that the empresses came from Syria, so that many of the rulers were partly Syrian, and devoted special religious attention to that country. As regards Heliopolis, inscriptions and coins demonstrate that the monumental forecourt and Propylaeum date from the time of Caracalla, though they were not completed until somewhat later.

Plate 30 The theatre at Sabratha (Alinari) Sabratha benefited largely from the vast building activity of Septimius in his native north Africa.

The outstanding single monument of Sabratha is, of course, the late-second-century theatre, outstanding not so much because it was in any way unusual in its own day as because the discovery and accurate restoration to its full height of the façade of the stage-building has made it possible to appreciate the visual subtleties of one of these elaborate columnar façades in a way that is quite impossible from even the best paper restorations.

All that is missing is the coffered wooden ceiling, cantilevered forward over the stge, and the facing of marble veneer that covered the wall surfaces behind the columns. . . .

The stage-building. . . . [incorporates] an outer ambulatory corridor, and [was] embellished externally with a triple order in low relief, both features that go back to the Roman tradition represented by the Theatre of Marcellus [13 or 11 BC].

(JBWP, p. 380)

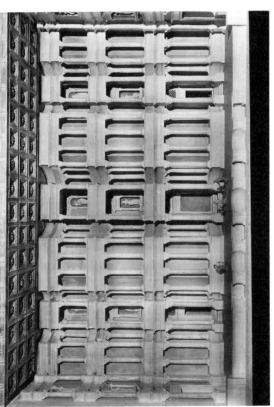

Plate 31 The Baths of Caracalla, Rome (Anderson)

Although very fragmentary, this is the largest and most imposing of all remains of ancient Rome, and is still in use today to house operas and other performances, although audiences have found it somewhat disconcerting when huge fragments of the ancient structure fly off the main fabric and fall to the ground.

As is stated in the text, J. B. Ward-Perkins sees the Baths as the embodiment of Roman concrete architecture at its moment of full maturity.

Plate 32 The Arch of Caracalla at Cuicul (Djemila) in north Africa (Alinari)

The Roman imperial custom of erecting Triumphal Arches spread from the capital to the provinces, and particularly, under the Severi, to their home country of north Africa.

One African place which received such an Arch was Cuicul (Djemila), a town cunningly laid out at the northern end of a narrow plateau steeply rising above two valleys. A military colony since AD 96/7, Cuicul grew wealthy and expanded in the only possible direction, that is to say southwards. This expansion was signalized and formalized by the creation of a second and more substantial Forum outside the original walls, dominated by an Arch of Caracalla (216) – shown here – and a Temple of the Severan House, apparently dating from the reign of Severus Alexander (229) (Chapter 3, n. 1, Chapter 5, n. 3). The Arch opens on the road to Sitifis (Sétif). It is called *arcus triumphalis* on its inscription.

9

THE LAWYERS

Another of the remarkable features of the epoch is that, despite its disorders and miseries, there were first-class lawyers in extremely prominent positions, notably as coopted members of the imperial Council. They prompted a good deal of valuable humanitarian legislation, and were ultimately responsible for considerable social mobility (diminished by the distinction between *honestiores* and *humiliores*, Chapter 5).

Moreover, not only did the praetorian prefects serve as judges (Chapter 2), but the emperors themselves took a great deal of interest in the law. Very often, with the help of a jurist (serving, perhaps, as *a libellis*, the official charged with receiving petitions), it was they who gave the final verdicts in courts of law. It was probably not true that Septimius had been a pupil of Marcus Aurelius's lawyer Quintus Cervidius Scaevola.[1] But Septimius was deeply concerned with the law (Chapters 11, 12) – like his Parthian counterparts (Chapter 5) – and particularly with appeals and civil cases; and his imperial pronouncements (*constitutiones*: cf. n. 4 below) show legal skill.

His son Caracalla was said to be slack about legal hearings (*cognitiones*). But he, too, employed jurists on his Council. He seems to have initiated 'indulgences', perhaps in order to emulate Alexander III the Great. His successor Macrinus had been a conscientious lawyer. And Severus Alexander took a great interest in litigation.

One of the leading lawyers of the age was Aemilius Papinianus – Papinian.[2] It is uncertain what country Papinian originated from. His home country may have been Africa, or he could have been Syrian, from Emesa (Homs). At all events, after possibly being a pupil of Quintus Cervidius Scaevola (cf. above, n. 1), he enjoyed a successful official career. In 203 he became praetorian prefect,[3] in which capacity two other extremely eminent lawyers, Paulus and Ulpian (see below), served on his staff as assessors. But when Caracalla murdered Geta in 212 Papinian was shocked, and let it be known. So Caracalla ordered that he should be arrested and (like Geta's other supporters) executed.

Papinian's main works were thirty-seven books of *Quaestiones*, completed before 198, and nineteen books of *Responsa* (*Prudentium*), finished after 204. The *Quaestiones* deal with problems and doctrine, whereas the other book includes pronouncements made by the emperor (sometimes in the form of his legal rulings, *constitutiones*)[4] and by praetorian prefects, and other jurists. Papinian also composed other works, but was not the author of any systematic or comprehensive study.

He wrote very tersely – too much so, sometimes, for those who want to read with ease – and was informative, precise and elegant. His judgments, based on practical expertise, were his own. He was independent and judicial. These qualities caused him to propound original solutions, which were not limited by technicalities but left room for moral and equitable considerations – as well as for changes of mind, to which he was not averse. He was later held in great repute.

It is equally unknown where Julius Paulus came from. He was certainly a pupil of Quintus Cervidius Scaevola. Then, after a period as a practical advocate, he became, as we saw, one of the assessors of Papinian, when the latter was praetorian prefect. Subsequently Paulus was a member of the imperial Councils of Septimius Severus and Caracalla. Sent into exile by Elagabalus, he was brought back by Severus Alexander. It is uncertain whether he became praetorian prefect; perhaps he did, as a colleague of Ulpian. It is not clear when or where he died.

Paulus wrote very extensively. His works included sixteen books of *Ad Sabinum* (a description of the civil law, addressed to the memory of Masurius Sabinus, the founder of the Sabinian school of law (first century AD)), as well as a detailed examination, in eighty books, of the *Edict* (one of the most important sources of law), twenty-three books of *Responsa* and twenty-six books of *Quaestiones*, as well as notes and commentaries on Papinian and earlier jurists, and a large number of monographs upon legal subjects of many different kinds. And Paulus was best known subsequently – and very well known – because of his *Sententiae*, which form a useful collection of excerpts from his writings, dating from the beginnings of the fourth century AD.

Paulus displays wide interests, and is by no means uncritical or unoriginal. But his logical and keen intellect causes him on occasion to rationalize and brush aside practical considerations, so that he exhibits a certain dogmatic hardening of formerly elastic and pliable ideas. Although by nature a synthesizer, he cannot justly be accused of plagiarism. He relates discussions at the imperial Council in which he himself took part. But he insists that the emperor should obey the laws; this was perhaps Severus Alexander's reaction against Caracalla.

Domitius Ulpianus, Ulpian, came of a family which had long been settled at Tyre (Es-Sur) in Phoenicia (western Syria). Together with his fellow-lawyer Paulus, he served as assessor to Papinian, when the latter was praetorian prefect. Moreover, he held other offices as well, in addition to serving on the imperial Council. The details and successive stages of Ulpian's career are disputed. But it appears that he was *a libellis* (master of petitions) to the emperor Caracalla. Yet he was then sent into exile by Elagabalus, like Paulus. However, after the accession of Severus Alexander, Ulpian became prefect of the grain supply, and then one of three praetorian prefects. But the praetorian guard disliked his strict discipline and his desire to institute reforms, and murdered him, perhaps in 223, or possibly five years later – for he did not have a sufficiently strong imperial protector, unlike Papinian. After Ulpian's death, his proposed reforms were abandoned. And the custom of having jurists as praetorian prefects (which had never been invariable) was dropped, in favour of a return to military men.

Ulpian wrote a very great deal, mostly during the reign of Caracalla. His principal works were *Ad Sabinum* (the reference is, once again, to the first-century jurist Masurius Sabinus), in fifty-one books, and an eighty-one-book essay on *The Edict* (see above, on Paulus), with a two-book appendix on *The Edict of the Curule Aediles*. In these works he aimed at a comprehensive restatement of the various interpretations of civil and edictal law. Ulpian also wrote monographs and guides for lawyers (for example seven books of legal rules (*regulae*)), and other text-books, as well as collections of opinions.

Like Paulus, Ulpian was, above all, an encyclopaedic compiler. His purpose was to sum up the achievements of his predecessors, with whose works he displayed a noteworthy familiarity, accompanied by salutary criticism. Ulpian may have been less incisive and original than Paulus, and more bureaucratically inclined. But he was clear, unaffected and reliable, and wrote with ease. Disregarding the current distinction between *honestiores* and *humiliores*, he maintained that everyone is equal before the Natural Law – except the emperor, who, he asserted (and this was a modification of Paulus), was on certain occasions outside and exempted from the law.[5] Nearly a third of the *Digest* is derived from Ulpian's writings – more than twice as much as what comes from Paulus.[6]

These three men, Papinian, Paulus and Ulpian, exercised more influence on the future than anyone else of the time, including the emperors (with the possible exception of novelists, Chapter 10). Whatever part the lawyers may or may not have played in the production of the *Constitutio Antoniniana* (Chapter 5), the Severan epoch, and its special spirit, are truly theirs.

10

THE NOVEL: LONGUS

Although education was officially encouraged, there is rather a startling lack of good literature in Severan times, apart from what the
lawyers wrote. In Latin there is virtually nothing (except among
the Christians in Africa, Chapter 12). But one must suspect – and
emphasize, since history is not solely a question of emperors and their
eccentricities but also of social life – that the upper classes at least
read a good deal of Greek fiction, in which the writers took an
interest in experimenting with literary forms. Philostratus might
perhaps be described as a fiction-writer, although his purpose was
primarily religious.

As for the other writers of fiction, however, the novelists or
authors of romances, they need to be considered against their background, which was Sophistic. The original Sophists of Socrates's day
had been itinerant lecturers who earned a living by teaching young
men how to get on in life: they were the equivalent of modern
correspondence courses. After the first century AD, however, a new
type of Sophist came into existence. This was the expert on rhetoric,
who worked partly as a teacher, partly as an advocate in the law
courts, and partly as a public entertainer. Rohde suggested that
Sophists of this type were responsible for effecting a synthesis
between the story of love and the story of travel. And so, according
to him, they invented the novel.

> Several other theories have been put forward to account for the
> sudden appearance of this very individual form of composition.
>
> Some have pointed out . . . that the novel was primarily the
> offspring of a marriage between Hellenism and Orientalism.
> Others have stressed the fact that some of the novels, like *The
> Ephesiaca* [of Xenophon] and *The Aethiopica* [of Heliodorus]
> have geographical titles. And this has been used to support a
> theory that the *genre* developed from the local legends of Magna

Graecia, Greece itself, the Greek islands, and Asia Minor. Others again have found the origin of the novel in the semi-mythical anecdotes that grew up round historical characters during the Alexandrian Age.[1]

The tendency of recent criticism, however, has not been to postulate any single source for the Greek novel, but rather to consider all the early Greek elements which may jointly have contributed, directly or indirectly, to the growth of this new literary form.

In this connection, Paul Turner cites *The Odyssey*, Euripides, Herodotus, Xenophon (the historian), Menander, Apollonius Rhodius, Aristides of Miletus and Parthenius. But he adds that one of the authors of romance, Longus, is a better writer, and more intelligent, than the other novelists. He also points, aptly, to the sense of humour of Longus. In his *Daphnis and Chloe*, he has taken over the slightly sickly love stories of his predecessors, but, in so doing, he also makes fun of them. Surely that is the only way in which we can take the prolonged inability of Daphnis and Chloe to make love to one another (see below). Longus was also a man of considerable insight into human affairs.[2]

It is usually hard to date these novelists, despite the enormous fame that many of them later attained. This difficulty is accentuated by the fact that many of them seem to have been at deliberate pains to make their efforts timeless. But Chariton, Iamblichus, Xenophon of Ephesus and Achilles Tatius seem too early for the present book; and Heliodorus of Emesa (despite doubts) is perhaps too late.[3] It does appear likely, however – though still not entirely certain – that Longus's novel belongs to this period. N. Holzberg writes:

> Everything points to Longus as the conscious imitator [of an earlier novelist, Achilles Tatius], trying at the same time to outdo his predecessor. This at least provides us with a fairly reliable *terminus post quem* for the novel. . . .
>
> We may place it at the earliest towards the end of the second century, a dating also suggested by various associative links with contemporary works of art,[4] as well as stylistic and thematic similarities to other literature of the age. It cannot, on the other hand, be assigned to a period too far into the third century. . . . Longus's work, we may then assume, was written around the turn of the second to the third century.[5]

Longus may well have come from Lesbos, where his novel is

located. It is possible that he was one of the Pompeii Longi, a family which we find in inscriptions on the island.[6]

Longus begins his novel by giving an account of Mytilene, the capital city of the island of Lesbos. He describes a rural property some miles away, briefly sketching the lush environment in which the action of his novel will take place. Daphnis and Chloe, we are told, were discovered as foundlings in the middle of this scenery. Readers were familiar with stories of the recognition of a single exposed child by means of birth-tokens. But the problem confronted by Longus involves two such children. He faces this double question with equanimity, and duly tells us how a goatherd comes upon Daphnis, already a large boy, suckled by a goat, while a shepherd finds Chloe suckled by a sheep, which licks her face clean.

Next, we learn that the two of them have become 15 and 13 years of age, at which point their foster-fathers dream dreams sent to them by Eros (Love), who instructs them to set the juvenile pair to jobs in the fields. The two foster-fathers are not very happy about these directions, since the birth-tokens had caused them to hope for something better than their own humble station for the children. But they comply all the same, and Daphnis and Chloe start to work in their idealized rural surroundings.

Once there, they have their first quasi-sexual encounter. Daphnis falls into a wolf-trap, and Chloe helps to get him out − employing her bra as a rope, and then seeing him wash himself after the accident, an experience which gives her a sensation she has not had before. Then Daphnis, too, becomes conscious of Chloe, when she gives him a casual kiss, after he has had a contest with a certain Dorcon. But now Dorcon disguises himself as a wolf (reminiscent of the wolf-trap into which Daphnis had fallen), in order to frighten Chloe and get closer to her. Before he is able to take any action, however, he is attacked by her dogs. But meanwhile, he has given her presents; though Chloe believes they came not from Dorcon, but from Daphnis.

The next threat to the youthful pair comes from pirates, whose role in such matters was traditional. They were thwarted, in this case, because their ship turned turtle, since Chloe's performance with the pipes so greatly captivated the oxen on board that they crowded on one side to hear her, thus overturning the ship. Dorcon, too (now dying), played the pipe, and this helped Daphnis to escape and swim to shore, while the pirates were dragged down in the water by a weir.

From now on, Longus describes the sexual arousal of this innocent couple. First they proceed a little further along that path when they meet the old gardener Philetas, at the vintage celebrations. Then Chloe is again captured by another set of pirates, whereupon, once she has escaped by a prayer to the god Pan, she and Daphnis have at least reached the age when they can exchange oaths of mutual loyalty. Philetas offers them an ancient piece of advice about how they should now proceed, observing that it is up to older people to pass on the secrets of human procreation to the younger generation. Daphnis and Chloe, however, are merely confused. Moreover, they are now distracted by hostilities that break out between the Lesbian town of Methymna (from which a group of noble picnickers have got involved in a quarrel with some herdsmen), and the herdsmen in question. Through the arbitration of the god Pan, the Methymnaeans, who have sent a fleet and seized Chloe, are persuaded to give her back. The war has come to an end, and is followed by rural festivities, at which she and Daphnis perform an improvised pantomime. But the two now fall out with one another, though Pan and Philetas do their best to bring them together again. Yet they fail, and in Book III Daphnis has an affair with an older woman, while Chloe proposes to marry someone else – a wealthy suitor.

Next, we revert to the Methymnaeans and their war, which has come to an end, as we saw – it has come to an end because they considered that peace would be more profitable for themselves. At this point, however, Daphnis and Chloe are reunited, owing to a curious accident. This is in winter, and when spring comes again their mutual attraction reasserts itself more actively still, although they still have no idea what to do. Another woman, Lycaenion, offers the necessary explanations to Daphnis. But Chloe is meanwhile once again being urged by other suitors to marry not him, but themselves. Daphnis, however, is provided with the necessary dowry by the nymphs, and despite a little lovers' quarrel all seems set fair, provided that the owner of the estate, Dionysophanes, agrees. At this point emerges the fact that the birth-tokens of both Daphnis and Chloe indicate that each of them is of aristocratic origin. They duly get married, and at the end of the novel it appears that the marriage is consummated.[7]

Unlike the heroes and heroines of earlier novels, Daphnis and Chloe do not have many exciting adventures, or travel far afield. For Longus, apparently, had quite other factors in mind.

It is difficult to resist the feeling [writes J. R. Morgan] that these atrophied incidents are intended as dead-pan caricatures of conventional romantic adventures. . . . In the area of love Longus is clearly reacting critically against the generic stereotype. . . .

Longus's thought world seems to revolve round the sequential harmonization of opposites, regardless of conventional evaluation. . . . It is hardly surprising that [*Daphnis and Chloe*] is preoccupied with its own status and function as a fiction, and the relation between fiction and experience in general.[8]

I think Morgan has got hold of a good point, when he concludes, at the beginning of this passage, that Longus is deliberately getting away from, if not actually making fun of, the romantic sentimentality of earlier novels.[9] He parades his debts to the pastoral tradition founded by Theocritus (perhaps the novel was originally called *Poimenika*, 'pastoral story'), and positively flaunts the unreality in which this dependence results. Yet the doings of his hero and heroine – and particularly their prolonged unawareness of the sexuality which their relationship is going to involve – look like jokes at the expense of his romantic predecessors. And he seems to make this clear, by what he says.

'We tried kissing', they thought, 'and it was no use. We tried embracing, and got nothing out of it. Apparently the only cure for love is lying down together. We must try that too. There must be something in it that will be more effective than kissing' . . .

Well, the kissing took place and the embracing went with it. But they were rather slow about trying the third remedy, since Daphnis did not dare to suggest it and Chloe did not like to take the initiative – until, quite by accident, they tried that too. . . . They lay for a long time as if they had been tied together. But as they had no idea what to do next and thought that love could go no further, nothing came of it. . . .

[Later, however, Daphnis, who had been] sitting drearily at home . . . was far more bold and enterprising about the whole business. . . . Lycaenion began to educate Daphnis . . . [and] Nature herself taught Daphnis all that remained to be done. . . . Daphnis did some of the things that Lycaenion had taught him; and then for the first time Chloe realised that what had taken place on the edge of the wood had been nothing but childish play.[10]

Hitherto the lovers have been kept apart by psychological as well as physical means, in spite of the advice of Philetas (cf. above); but now they come together.

We have to envisage a large readership which needed fiction to take its mind off the horrors of the period but was, by now, discontented with the simpler stories that earlier writers had provided for them. People of this Severan age wanted something sharper and more pungent. In satisfying such requirements, Longus is deliberately criticizing and trying to outdo his forerunners such as Achilles Tatius, as we saw above. And it is quite right to conclude that the way in which he does so is a masterpiece of intuitive perception.[11] His prologue, which strikes an unusual note among Greek novels, is complex,[12] but elegant. It explains, not altogether sincerely, that the work is based on a painting,[13] and adds that it explains that Longus's story is 'a simple votive offering to Love[14] – with the elusive touch that the author prays for restraint and sanity in describing its operations: a prayer granted to few of his fellow-novelists. So here too Longus is criticizing his predecessors.

He has rightly been described as the most marked individualist among the writers of Greek novels.[15] His style, though generally simple, displays a mannered balance that rises to poetical, incantatory, idiosyncratic, mesmeric heights.

> He has [writes Peter Levi] a voyeuristic streak, and has attracted fine illustrations, as well as some vulgar ones, in modern times. But he is never obscene. His theme is the pleasure and innocence of love, his characters being of such rustic innocence that the pleasure is long delayed.
>
> His style sparkles with charm and amusement, and his Greek is attractively readable. . . . Of all the late Greek writers, Longus is the one that students most infallibly enjoy. He is a sorbet of literature. He melts on analysis, and there seems nothing to him. But he gives great pleasure. . . . The story and the style are trembling on the edge of over-sweetness and childishness. They have a pantomime quality. Yet they are saved by humour and by a certain sprinkling of saltiness.
>
> *Daphnis and Chloe* is well written; it is a beautiful and a

unique achievement. . . . So late in their history, it is evident that the ancient Greeks had entirely lost neither their virtuosity nor their originality.[16]

11

ART AND ARCHITECTURE

The characteristically Roman method of depicting the emperor's achievements upon a relief had already found important expression in Augustus's Altar of Peace, the Arch of Titus in the Roman Forum, Trajan's Column in the Forum of Trajan and the Column of Marcus Aurelius in Rome's Piazza Colonna.

The reliefs of the Arch of Septimius Severus in the Forum at Rome (AD 203, Plate 27) are worse preserved than those of the Column of Marcus, but not entirely different in character. Yet there has been a development, for the figures are more squat; and an intricate division between scenes, shown in a bird's-eye perspective, conveys the impression of a textile surface. Probably this sort of pattern was inspired by popular paintings, now vanished, such as those which Septimius exhibited at his Parthian Triumph.

His Arch at Lepcis Magna (c. 203, Plate 28) has a panel depicting a siege by the same map-like, spatial narrative method. Another scene on the Lepcis monument, showing the ruler in his chariot, introduces a novel and almost medieval technique, two-dimensional rather than plastic, that concentrates upon rhythmical, repetitive symmetry and rigid frontality.

This principal of symmetry, which increasingly gains artistic favour from now on, had already been favoured on certain Roman medallions. In due course, symmetrical, balanced composition became as normal on Roman coinage as the schematic fire-altars on coins of Sassanian Persia.

Some of the artists of the Lepcis Arch have been traced to a long-lived school of sculpture at Aphrodisias (Gehre) in Caria. But the emphatically frontal presentation of the imperial figure, which recurs on the small Arch of the Bankers at Rome (AD 204), comes from a good deal further east than Aphrodisias, being typical of the fringe regions between the Roman and Parthian empires. Frontality had, it is true, been seen before on Greek and Roman reliefs and coins. But this stiff hieratic posture clearly recalls saviour-gods at Palmyra (Tadmor) in the Syrian desert, and at Dura-Europus and Hatra (al-Hadr) in Mesopotamia. Many centuries earlier there had already been frontal portraiture in western Persian lands; and Parthian kings are sometimes shown facing the spectator, like potent talismanic images. Another contemporary analogy seems to have been the Greco-Buddhist art of northern India. This is very close to Palmyrene work. It presumably came westwards by sea via the Persian Gulf.

The chariot on the Arch of Lepcis is partly frontal and partly in profile. But coinage shows how such chariot scenes rapidly assumed a complete heraldic frontality, first in the eastern provinces and then later in the west and at Rome itself. When the Lepcis relief shows the central, frontal Septimius among other figures, he – even more emphatically than Marcus Aurelius on his earlier Column – is united not with them but with the reverential spectators, at whom he is gazing as the Boddhisatva gazed at his worshippers.

This is an onslaught upon the emotions rather than an approach to the mind, a spiritual revolution that led to the frontal, symmetrical mosaics of the Byzantine age.[1]

The imperial portraiture of the Severan age shows what was going on.

Septimius, in order to conceal the advent of grimmer times, reverted to propaganda recalling the Golden Age of the Antonines, whom he claimed as his ancestors in spirit and by adoption. . . . His portrait-busts[2] go back to Marcus Aurelius and Lucius Verus, but with certain technical and psychological changes. Volumes are more solid, the lavish hair with the curls of the god Serapis is closely integrated with the skull, and in anticipation of future styles the eyes (incised since early in the second century) are sometimes raised to heaven, gazing with exalted emotion at the gods who were the emperor's companions. . . .

The portrait-busts of the Syrian ladies of Septimius's house[3] display a new, subtle and confident sensibility which reflects their strong, un-Roman characters, and political and intellectual power. Picturesque coiffures help to make sinuous or geometric patterns of line and form. The disturbing turn of these heads and eyes reinforces the suggestion, apparent in some of the heads of Septimius, that the spirit, a mere alien sojourner in the human frame, can be detected behind and beyond its features. Self-contained and self-centred humanism is coming to an end.

Among the most remarkable portraits of the age are the nervous, scowling, Alexander-emulating busts of Caracalla, with restless head and wrinkled brow; an outstanding example of the baroque portraitists' new kind of face, stamped by destiny, excitement and violence.[4]

This is no longer a philosopher on the throne. Although his official name was Marcus Aurelius Antoninus, Caracalla's harsh violence has abandoned the Antonine synthesis in favour of a more excitable and defiant self-assertion. Hellenic locks, too, have been replaced by short neat curls, which eastern local coinages also now begin to show in stylised patterns.

A marble bust, which may represent Caracalla's murdered brother Geta, makes this hair-style into a close-cropped skull-cap, symbolising military puritanism against Hellenic culture, according to a convention which became widely accepted in the years ahead.

Portrait-busts of Severus Alexander . . . sketch this sheath-like hair and beard with light, rapid, pointillist strokes of the chisel, drawing upon the illusionistic techniques of painting, with the aid of tints to flesh and hair which have now vanished. Naturalistic and schematic tendencies are balanced one against the other. And it is just this balance and tension that gives the portraits of this age their claim to be the most remarkable (as well as the most accessible to modern taste?) that Rome ever produced.

In contrast to the heads of Elagabalus, which are soft, rounded, chinless and juvenile (Plate 16),[5] the portraits of Severus Alexander, to which reference has been made here, show not only novel, close-cropped hair but also a new sort of geometric structure.[6]

Painting was another art which was by no means inactive under the Severi.[7]

As for sarcophagi, they had already during the preceding period become of major artistic importance, reflecting contemporary interest in achieving victory, in the after-life and eternity. And now,

such concern was intensified, stressing allegorical, mystical myth-
ology, in various shapes. These prestigious, costly coffins or sarcophagi were made not only at Rome, but also at Athens, and close
to sculptural quarries such as those at Aphrodisias and other centres
of Asia Minor.

In keeping with their varied origins and locations, the sarcophagi
also assumed various shapes. There was an Attic form, an Asiatic
form and a Roman or western form.

In the history of art, these sarcophagi became increasingly pre-
dominant, replacing and superseding other artistic media, and attract-
ing the talents of the best Roman, Greek and eastern craftsmen and
artists of successive generations. Indeed, these men made such burial
monuments the principal vehicles for the sculptural ornament and
pattern-making of the empire. This sort of relief sculpture had
already attained excellence in the time of Hadrian (AD 117–38), and
thereafter continued to grow rapidly. The artists had the Roman
market in view: in Greece and Asia Minor alike (as well as Italy,
where some of these sculptors went), from a slightly later date, a
number of independent workshops were producing abundant sarcophagi for rich Roman clients. And so, in the history of Roman
sculpture, the sarcophagi of this period play a role of major significance – even if artistic masterpieces of the first quality are rare.

Asian-style sarcophagi had already been a prominent artistic feature
in the preceding epoch. And now they reached the zenith of diversity
and technique, in c. 220. They display, in contrast to the perpetuated
classicism of Attic styles, deep drillings and sharp outlines, reflecting
an elegant elaboration dissolving in strong plastic effects of light and
shade.

A. W. Lawrence describes one of their masterpieces, found near
Sidamara (Sidamaria) in Lycaonia and now at Istanbul, and comments
on such sarcophagi in the following terms:

> Their plan results in a fusion of the Greek tomb-shape and
> the Italian design of a flat-topped chest bearing a recumbent
> figure. . . .
>
> Excessive use of the drill, which produces violent juxta-
> positions of light and shade, and transforms classical mouldings
> into nothing better than vermiculation, results from the Roman
> taste for pictorial rather than sculptural effects.
>
> Repeated anti-classic tendencies in imperial art are expressed
> in the taste for a continuous motive without beginning or end,

like an arabesque, as against the ancient use of the independent and fully developed incident. Every available space of the background is covered with decoration.[8]

The themes of these sarcophagus reliefs are various. But there is great stress, not unnaturally, upon victory in the after-life. Most people hoped for better times in the life to come. In the 'philosopher sarcophagi' this other-worldly aim is obvious: we have been placed within the realm of higher values. Battle-pieces and hunting scenes (including the famous Ludovisi Sarcophagus, Chapter 12, n. 1), neither entirely unprecedented, allegorically symbolize the search of the dead man's soul for success in eternity. And so do sarcophagi in the Capitoline and Vatican museums depicting the career of Achilles, with its mystical implications, and other reliefs showing the Labours of Hercules (Chapter 12, nn. 1, 9). Such themes gave a fine opportunity to artists, while at the same time forming part of the endeavour to retain Greco-Roman paganism as the unique religion of the western world (Chapter 12).

After a fire in one of the last years of Commodus (191), Rome was virtually rebuilt by Septimius Severus and Julia Domna. Many ancient monuments were restored by the emperors and members of their house, private initiatives being less prominent than heretofore, owing to economic pressures. The 151 slabs of the Marble Plan of Rome proudly record this imperial achievement, although the historian Dio Cassius says it included a good deal of wastefulness.[9]

The Palatine Hill at Rome figured prominently in the programme. As John Ward-Perkins observed,

> The Severan work on the Palatine . . . was directed principally towards the development of the southern corner of the hill, extending in this direction the already existing Flavian Palace. . . . It involved the building of a whole new wing, terraced out above massive arched substructures. . . .
>
> All too little has survived of the buildings that stood upon them at the level of the main palace. But that little suffices to show in places an almost frightening disregard for the disposition of the walls and vaults beneath. The architect of this wing was very sure both of his materials and of his own ability to use them. . . .
>
> The largest single enterprise of Septimius Severus's reign had been the restoration and extension of the Palace.

This enterprise amounted to the creation of an entire new terraced wing of the Flavian Palace (Domus Augusta).[10]

The most singular of the Severan buildings on the Palatine was the Septizodium (Septizonium), a lofty decorative façade dedicated by Septimius Severus in 203. . . . It took the form of an elaborate columnar screen, three orders high, and in plan consisting of three apsed recesses flanked by two shallow rectangular wings, the free-standing equivalent of the stage-building of a contemporary theatre. It was probably equipped as a fountain. And the name[11] suggests a symbolic association with the seven planets. Architecturally its only function was as a screen concealing the buildings behind.

The nearest analogies to it are the *nymphaea* that were used for precisely this purpose in many cities of Asia Minor during the first and second centuries AD.

This Septizodium or Septizonium at Rome, destroyed by Domenico Fontana in 1588/9, was intended to give a monumental front to the imperial Palace where it faced the Via Appia (Appian Way), so as to meet the eyes of travellers from Africa. The association with the seven planets, suggested by Ward-Perkins, is not unlikely, especially in view of Septimius's own superstitious beliefs (Chapter 1), which were widely shared. And his statue on this monument probably displayed him as Sun-god, with the seven planets around him (Chapter 12). He also judged cases in the Septizodium (Chapter 9). It is possible that its façade, reminiscent of a stage background, was divided into more zones than Ward-Perkins envisaged, that is to say into seven zones or apses, representing, like the name of the building, the planets, and each containing the statue of a planetary divinity. This façade was adorned by columns of African marble and granite echoing the architecture of Asia Minor.

Triumphal Arches were another form of architecture or art which reached a climax during this period.

The Roman ability to use concrete for the making of arches led . . . to the single, independent, free-standing arch. . . . Such arches, incorporating ever more complex ornamental themes and sculptures, became the symbols of empire, and of heroic conquest. . . .

These arches did not play any functional role in the external defences of a city, for which, indeed, their openness would have served no purpose. Crowned by bronze statues of emperors or gods, often in horse-drawn chariots – although all this statuary cannot, usually, be seen today since it has vanished a long time ago – the Triumphal Arches [were a perpetual reminder] of the power and grandeur of Rome.[12]

The Arch of Septimius Severus at Rome is a much more elaborate affair than the Arch of Titus [AD 79–81], at the opposite end of the Forum. Seventy-five feet high and eighty-two feet wide, it is large enough to have its interior divided into several vaulted chambers reached by an internal staircase. Moreover, the arch does not have just one single opening, but three, in accordance with a custom that came from the Greek east, where there was a tradition of multiple monumental gateways.

The Arch of Severus, like the Arch of Titus, is built of Pentelic marble. Owing to the passage of centuries it stood higher than the ground level of the Republic. And the artificial, stepped base of the arch raised it to an even greater height.

The base also meant that there could be no question of processions passing under it as they had passed under Titus's Arch. The monument of Severus had no such function. . . . It was originally crowned by statues of the emperor and his sons in a chariot of six horses, with further equestrian statues to right and left. . . . Shields and other metal ornaments or trophies were attached to it.

The purpose of the monument, indicated in a long inscription repeated on each of its frontages, was to celebrate the victories of Septimius and his sons and colleagues Caracalla and Geta over the Parthians and their allies in Mesopotamia and Assyria (AD 195–9). The emperors had allegedly 'restored the Roman state and extended its empire'. . . . The occasion chosen for this celebration was the tenth anniversary of the reign (203). (The name of Septimius's younger son Geta . . . is no longer to be seen. . . . For Caracalla assassinated Geta, and ordered the erasure of his name from all official inscriptions. . . .)

Much the most important reliefs are those in the large frontal panels above the lateral arches. Unfortunately, however, they are ill-preserved. . . . Each of the four panoramas, as now interpreted, is concerned with a single Mesopotamian city (or in one case two cities) that provided an episode in the wars. . . .

The reliefs do not follow the *continuous* narrative method of the two Columns [of Trajan and Marcus Aurelius]. This . . . is not a flowing epic but a series of high-lighted and always significant dramatic acts. . . .

It is possible to detect a stylistic development: a further move away from classicism. . . . Individual human beings have become squat and insignificant, they are intended to stand for crowds rather than persons. Grouped in ceremonial tableaux which are dominated by the emperors who declaim to their serried ranks, the figures take on the undulating rhythm of a single undifferentiated mass. . . . Times were changing.[13]

The three passageways of the Arch of Septimius Severus in the Roman Forum have coffered vaulting. Its reliefs include a remarkable bird's-eye view of a city. As for the work in general, it is clearly influenced by the Column of Trajan and his Arch at Beneventum (Benevento), and by the Column of Marcus Aurelius. However, the stocky, graceless figures (in so far as one can see them, in their badly damaged condition) are less rounded than those of the Column of Marcus Aurelius. It must be added that the crowded reliefs on the Arch of Septimius, renouncing classical formulae, somewhat obliterate the structure and upset its balance. The motifs are still Roman – Mars and Victory can be seen, along with Summer and Winter. But they have degenerated into extravagance.

Another Severan Arch at Rome is the Arch of the Bankers (Arcus Argentariorum), with its flat lintel, over a square aperture. The lintel is supported by two piers with broad, composite (mainly Corinthian) pilasters.

The little Arch that clings to the western wall of the portico of the church of San Giorgio in Velabro, between the Palatine and the Tiber . . . is known as the Porta Argentariorum, since an inscription states that it was dedicated to Septimius and his family in 204 by the bankers [money-changers] (*argentarii*) in collaboration with the wholesale cattle-dealers (*negotiantes boarii*).

[The two main] reliefs, as we see them now, are incomplete. For after the murders of Caracalla's father-in-law Plautianus in 205, of his wife Plautilla in 211, and of his brother Geta in 212, the portraits of the victims were removed.

One panel now shows Caracalla by himself, sacrificing at a tripod and virtually full-face, although his head is inclined slightly towards the spectator's left. In the other panel Septimius and his empress [Julia Domna] are also sacrificing at a tripod. Here Julia Domna is completely, Septimius very nearly, frontal. Both of them . . . gaze straight before them into the distance as though to scan the faces, and accept the homage, of the onlookers.

Noteworthy, too, is the flat, two-dimensional technique in which the figures are rendered.[14]

This Arch of the Bankers is an exception to the general custom, already mentioned, that the emperor, not the impoverished private citizens and public institutions, undertook building. But the themes of the reliefs are thoroughly imperial. And, as on the Arch of Septimius not far away, it may be complained that they swamp the structure, so as to make it scarcely visible.

A more imposing monument is the great four-way Arch of Septimius at Lepcis Magna (Lebda) in Tripolitana, one of many in Severan Africa (cf. n. 18 below).

It is [this] provincial monument . . . that provides the fullest and most exciting document of Severan historical sculpture. . . .

Its sculptured scenes are of local significance and refer to specific ceremonies enacted at Lepcis on the occasion of the visit of the imperial family to Septimius's native city [in 203–4].

These ceremonies seem to have been staged with two ends in view – first, to stress the glory won by Septimius through his victories in the east, and, secondly . . . to exhibit Caracalla in particular as the emperor's elder son, colleague, and destined successor. . . .

Of the four historical friezes that ran round the attic of the Arch three are reasonably well preserved. The most important of them presents the triumphal entry of Septimius into Lepcis. . . . The front of [his] chariot, and Septimius and his two sons standing in it, are completely full-face, as are also the personages walking at the horses' heads and the repetitive figures of bearded men, who, ranged in a serried row and reared above the foreground figures, watch the procession from the background as it passes by. . . . The imperial group has been deliberately pulled round to a frontal view in order to give it a hieratic aspect and rivet our attention upon it. . . . In another frieze, a scene of sacrifice in Julia Domna's honour, we find the same monotonous row of tiered, frontal onlookers in the background, while the figures in the foreground, if not all rigidly full-face, are basically frontal. . . .

Characteristic of all three friezes is the extensive use of drilling in the drapery and the almost wholly two-dimensional curving of the figures in the second plane. . . . [We have here] features with which western artists were as yet only experimenting – the extreme form of drill technique, with its highly patterned, black-and-white effects, and insistence on frontality, that recalls the 'Parthian' art of Palmyra, Dura-Europus and Hatra.[15]

Hurriedly erected, so it would seem, this Arch at Lepcis Magna was placed across the junction of the main street of the town and the coast road.

The reliefs are deeply cut, and (cf. above) two-dimensional. They are also much more hieratic than those on the Arch of Septimius at Rome. There is a kind of incorporeal illusionism, an exploration of impressionistic, dematerialized, optical effects, a rhythmical, repetitive symmetry. The sculptors are Asian, and there is also evidence of African influence, since Lepcis Magna was in Africa and Septimius came from Africa and Lepcis, so that we see depictions of the African gods Hercules and Bacchus (as on coins; cf. Ward-Perkins below, and Chapter 12).

For in addition to undertaking important military building in many other provinces, the emperor Septimius Severus enriched his home town of Lepcis Magna not only with this Arch, but with many other buildings as well (as we shall see). One of them was a huge Basilica (dedicated by Caracalla in 216).

[Septimius's] Basilica at Lepcis Magna was a vast colonnaded hall, with a central, ornamented apse at each extremity. It was sixty-two feet wide, and there were galleries above the side aisles, giving a total height estimated at over one hundred feet. Along the north-eastern façade ran an enclosed street.

The façade itself was ornate and individual.

Pedestals were lavishly employed to provide additional height for this Basilica. In general, height, as well as grace, was stressed. And there was ample employment of first-class masonry, supplemented by the variegated use of brightly coloured marbles and elaborate, deeply incised, architectural ornamentation. Rings of acanthus foliage appeared between bases and columns.

It must be concluded that the Basilica at Lepcis Magna, and the other buildings of Severan date in the city, were probably designed by one single architect. . . .

[Non-Roman] details can be detected, but also a western, Roman spirit. The author's commission must have been to follow Roman models.[16]

We find, among the reliefs, Dionysus (Bacchus, Shadrap), the patron deity of Lepcis Magna – whose exploits are richly carved on the pilasters – and Hercules (Melkart), the patron of the Severan house (Chapter 12).

The buildings of Septimius Severus at Lepcis Magna also include a new colonnaded street beside a second Forum, 1,000 by 600 feet in dimension, which was flanked by shops, as well as by the Basilica just described. Septimius also rebuilt the city's port on a magnificent scale, though the scheme was apparently ineffective owing to silting. Vaulted Hunting Baths, dating from the third century, are still extant. A wall painting suggests that they were erected by a group of hunters who provided wild animals to the amphitheatres of Africa and Italy;[17] that is to say, like the Arcus Argentariorum at Rome, the Baths were unusually of private, not imperial origin.

The artists in the imperial city, as was mentioned above in connection with the Arch, came from Asia Minor. At Lepcis Magna, inspired by the local origin of the imperial house, they were entrusted with the creation of a whole new monumental quarter.

In the rest of north Africa, too, there was extensive Severan building,[18] as there was also in Syria, the homeland of Septimius's wife Julia Domna (Chapter 8).[19] Nor were other countries neglected.[20] Moreover, there were also important structures at Rome itself.

Caracalla built a new and splendid temple on the Quirinal in honour of [the Egyptian god] Serapis. . . . [It] is to be identified with a gigantic building on the western edge of the Quirinal, near the Piazza del Quirinale. . . . It stood within a rectangular enclosure. And the most singular feature of the design, dictated presumably by the desire for strict orientation, was that it was the rear (west) wall which dominated the composition, flanked by the ramps of a grandiose double stairway which led down the steep slopes to the Campus Martius, 70 feet below.

The temple itself . . . was unique among Roman temples in

having a façade of twelve columns. It was certainly of gigantic proportions, the heights of the shafts being recorded as 60 Roman feet with comparable capitals and entablature.

The alleged Egyptian affinities of the plan may be questioned. . . . [But] the most puzzling feature of the surviving remains is the strongly 'Asiatic' character of the ornament.[21]

This presumably was due to the employment of Asian artists at Rome. Caracalla also sponsored further extensive building in the capital,[22] as well as in other cities of the empire. His Baths at Rome became eternally famous.

Standardization, and a more concrete approach to genuine equality, was apparent in . . . the stupendous Baths which were inaugurated by Septimius Severus at Rome, but bear the name of his son Caracalla who completed them.

There were finally eleven such public Baths in the capital, and smaller replicas and variants in almost every town of the empire. They displayed much ingenious multiplicity of function, being designed not only for luxurious bathing at various temperatures, but also for all the diverse social activities of an elaborate community centre, in which many people, belonging to a wide spectrum of social and economic classes, spent a substantial part of each day.[23]

All the features that had appeared in thermal establishments of the earlier empire were to be seen on a massive scale in the Baths of Caracalla, enriched by every sort of novel elaboration. Surrounded by an enclosure containing gardens and open-air gymnasiums and art-collections, the main building was provided with vast unseen services of heating, water-supply and drainage, designed to deal with the needs of 1,600 bathers.

The bathing accommodation included a circular domed hot room. And the central feature of the whole complex was a great cross-vaulted central hall or concourse containing a swimming-pool. This hall, measuring 185 by 79 feet, is so large that men and women almost vanish inside its immensity.

For all its services to human comfort, this is the architecture not of humanism but of a new age in which the individual is one of a mass. A new age, too, is heralded by the architectural style, since the load of the intersecting vaults, with their increased span and assurance, is carried not on a row of independent columns but on only four enormous piers dividing the hall into three bays – vaults and piers alike being constructed of the concrete which made these lightly soaring buildings possible.[24]

The groined cross-vaulting in the great central hall of the Baths of Caracalla was upheld by concealed buttresses. There is some doubt, however, regarding the use to which this hall was put. It is generally described as a *tepidarium*, but some would prefer to call it a *frigidarium*, 'cold room', since it was unheated (it contained four basins). The circular, domed *caldarium*, 'hot room' (now ruined) at one end of the shorter axis – which was far larger than the Pantheon of Hadrian – contained huge windows.

Although the brick-built structure of the Baths of Caracalla – in common with earlier thermal establishments – displayed no unified elevation, the complex was tightly and rationally planned as a rigid, symmetrical oblong, with an interplay of thrust and counter-thrust. There was a subtle and assured use of light and colour in this soaring space.

A vast area, 566 yards square, had been levelled for the creation of these Baths of Caracalla, and many houses were removed. Unlike the Baths of Trajan (to which the architect, nevertheless, owed debts), Caracalla's Baths isolated the main building in the centre of a huge, colonnaded precinct (*peribolos*), which terminated in a large central apse (*exedra*), with smaller apses on either side.

There were extensive service quarters, and an intricate heating system and hydraulic plant. Capitals displayed splendid decoration, and there was an abundance of statues and mosaics. Some of this art dated from the time of Severus Alexander, under whom, after their dedication by Caracalla in 216 (following ten years' work), the Baths were completed.

There was an Arch of Macrinus (217) at Diana Veteranorum (Zama) in north Africa. And under Elagabalus building continued.

> In Rome, Elagabalus [built a] magnificent temple on the Palatine to house the cult-image of the Baal of Emesa, together with an adjoining garden and shrine of Adonis. . . . The Temple of Sol Invictus Elagabalus occupied the site of what had been the Aedes Caesarum on the east spur of the Palatine, opposite Hadrian's Temple of Venus and Rome.
>
> The platform is still a prominent landmark and the foun-

dations of the temple itself have been partly excavated, beside and beneath the church of San Sebastiano al Palatino. From these remains and from representations on coins it can be seen to have been a large (200–230 by 130 feet) hexastyle peripteral building standing within a rectangular porticoed enclosure, with a monumental entrance facing on to the Clivus Palatinus.

After Elagabalus's death it was rededicated to Jupiter the Avenger (Jup[p]iter Ultor).[25]

The successor of Elagabalus, Severus Alexander, was responsible for this rededication. He also built a Nymphaeum at Rome – it is not certain where – and restored a number of buildings, including the Baths of Nero (which he lit at night) and the Colosseum, which had been struck by lightning.[26]

For Rome was still the centre of the world – the *Roma aeterna* of a medallion of Severus Alexander.[27] Septimius's rebuilding of the city has already been mentioned; he was *Restitutor Urbis*.[28] And it was to the emperors themselves (unencumbered by the subservient senate) that all eyes were turned.

12

PAGANISM AND CHRISTIANITY

The age of the Severi witnessed two very important developments in paganism: the persistence of monotheistic views and the growth of syncretism, which imported Egyptian and Syrian religious motifs to Rome, with the encouragement, no doubt, of the Syrian Julia Domna, the wife of Septimius (Chapter 8). There was also a great deal of philosophy,[1] astrology, mysticism and superstition, with which, as well as with religion, the mind and heart of Septimius were thoroughly pervaded. The religious buildings of the period show the sort of paganism that prevailed (Chapter 11).

As to monotheism, it came to be increasingly felt that there was one god, who might as well be called Jupiter, and that the other Olympians were, as one could say, manifestations of that single deity. He should be worshipped with high-minded austerity. The most significant pagan writing of the time was the long, partly fictitious *Life of Apollonius of Tyana* (215–38) by Flavius Philostratus.[2]

That Philostratus was the best man to whom to entrust so important a task is doubtful. It is true that he was a skilled stylist and a practised man of letters, an art critic and an ardent antiquarian, as we may see from his other works. But he was a Sophist rather than a deep thinker, and though an enthusiastic admirer of the philosopher Pythagoras and his school, was so from a distance, regarding such learning rather through a wonder-loving atmosphere of curiosity, embellished by a lively imagination, than from a personal acquaintance with its discipline, or from a practical knowledge of those hidden forces of the soul with which the adepts of Pythagoreanism dealt. We have, therefore, to expect from Philostratus a sketch of the appearance of a thing by one outside, rather than an exposition of the thing itself from within.[3]

Yet, unmistakably, Apollonius, in the first century AD, had been a magical, noble and saintly holy man. And it is tempting to see in him the pagan answer to Jesus Christ. But any deliberateness in this link is now frowned upon, since it seems doubtful whether Philostratus had any knowledge of the Christian Gospels.[4] However, Severus Alexander was said to have eclectically cherished busts or statues of Apollonius, as well as Jesus, Abraham and Orpheus,[5] and it was typical of this cosmopolitan age that he should have done so.

Apollonius, it may be repeated, was an outstanding figure, even it the details provided by Philostratus are partly discounted.

> A series of exchanges of Apollonius with [the invented?] Damis and with others . . . display his formidable moral and intellectual strength.
>
> He has many sides: the ascetic philosopher who blends Socratic and Cynic with predominantly neo-Pythagorean stances; the encyclopaedic sage who knows that eunuchs can feel sexual desire, and can discourse on animal behaviour; the phil-Hellene who secures the rights of descendants of Eretrians transplanted to Cissia [in 490 BC] by Darius I (521–486 BC); the literary scholar who knows obscure poems composed by one Damophyle of Pera (Murtana) (surely bogus) in the tradition of Sappho, and later criticizes the rhetorical style of Dio Chrysostom of Prusa (Brusa). . . . Apollonius talks philosophy and aesthetics with the Indian king Phraotes. . . .
>
> Book 4 starts with visits to Greek cities of Ionia and Achaea, in which Apollonius combines the sharp reforming tongue of a Stoic or Cynic philosopher with a readiness to offer political advice characteristic of a Sophist [cf. below].[6]

In the early years of the Christian era, the memory of the great mystic Apollonius of Tyana moved through the known world of the time, teaching wisdom and leaving strange legends of his miracles wherever he passed. Many devotees considered him divine. G. R. S. Mead, who wrote a fine study of his life and work, says:

> With the exception of the Christ, no more interesting personage appears upon the stage of Western history in those early years. . . . There is much opinion, gossip and rumour to sort out from the story of Apollonius. . . . Alexander Severus, the son of Julia Mamaea, worshipped Apollonius. . . .
>
> Was Apollonius, then, a rogue, a trickster, a charlatan, a fanatic, a misguided enthusiast, or a philosopher, a reformer,

a conscientious worker, a true initiate, one of the earth's great ones? This each must decide for himself, according to his knowledge or his ignorance.

I for my part bless his memory, and would gladly learn from him, as he is.[7]

Whether Julia Domna really had much of a salon is, as we have seen (Chapter 8), scarcely known. Or at least if it existed, it failed to produce much in the way of good literature, despite official encouragement and an interest in literary experimentation. Only Longus, who does not seem to have had much to do with her, and the lawyers, were really good (Chapters 9, 10).

But something must be said in favour of Philostratus as well, whatever his defects. Certainly he, as he says himself, was close to Julia Domna (and to Caracalla as well) – though the part she played in sponsoring his writings has been disputed.

In any case, Philostratus liked a good story, and his *Heroicus* might be called a Greek novel.[8] But it could also be regarded as a religious work (like his equally fictional, closely linked *Life of Apollonius of Tyana*: see above). For the *Heroicus* is concerned with the hero–cult of Protesilaus, described by Homer as a commander at Troy, a cult which, we are told by Philostratus, a 'Thracian vintner', in contact with the ghost of Protesilaus, defends against an at first sceptical Phoenician, demonstrating the continued existence and power of the ancient heroes.

Philostratus, who could be defined as a member of the Second Sophistic movement that had already flourished under the Antonines, was well-educated, informative and technically able. The reasons why he composed his *Heroicus* have been much discussed. It does seem probable, however, that the work was partly written in order to please and support Caracalla and Julia Domna, who were greatly addicted to the cult of heroes, which seemed analogous to the current cult of the imperial family (served in the eastern cities by the priestly establishment known as the 'neocorate'). And this worship of heroes was encouraged by Caracalla's devotion to the super-hero Alexander III the Great.[9] Philostratus showed a marked sympathy for Rome, where the ancient heroes were much respected and revered. He was at the same time able to take a swipe at another author, 'Dictys Cretensis', whose *Ephemeris* was non-heroic and rationalistic.[10]

Pescennius Niger (Chapter 1) prepares us for the eastern influences that were brought to bear on the Severans, because his coins were replete with oriental motifs, more or less blended with Roman traditions.[11] As to the import of Egyptian divinities to Rome, they reached the zenith of their popularity under Septimius, even in official, metropolitan circles – which were now increasingly open to such influences. Septimius's portraits, as we have seen, display him with the forelocks of Serapis, in whom both he and his son Caracalla (who built him a great temple in the capital: Chapter 11), were deeply interested. Furthermore, the patrons of their home town Lepcis Magna (Dionysus, Bacchus, Shadrap) and of the Severan house (Hercules, Melkart) received honours, notably in the Secular Games at Rome in 204, as well as at Lepcis Magna itself. Meanwhile sarcophagi, too, bore ample witness to the keen pagan interest in the after-life (Chapter 11).

Monotheism was often identified with the worship of Sol or Helios (the Sun).

> There was a belief, during this same epoch, which much more nearly [than Neo-Platonism] competed with Christ for the control of the western world. This was the cult of the Sun, which was revered by millions of the inhabitants of the Roman empire. And its religion for a time even became the state worship. . . . There was an ever-increasing tendency to explain the other traditional deities in terms of the Sun, in all but monotheistic fashion. . . .
>
> The cult of this deity offered flattering analogies to the imperial régime and its resplendent, sun-like leaders. Under Septimius Severus, whose wife Julia Domna came from Syria where reverence for the Sun was especially strong, its worship almost took command of the whole state religion. . . .
>
> The Sun-cult could well have become the religion of the Mediterranean area for an indefinite period ahead. But it did not do so, in the end, because such a divinity was too impersonal, too lacking in urgent human appeal. Devotees of the Sun themselves felt that this excessive remoteness failed to satisfy their needs. And a branch of the cult came into vogue in order to respond to such yearnings. It was the worship of an ancient Iranian deity, Mithras, who was god of the Morning Light, and . . . was identified with the Sun himself.
>
> But unlike the solar cult the ritual of Mithras always retained

its private character . . . in marked contrast to the Sun's innumerable appearances on the official coinage. . . . [So] it was Christianity, instead, that won the day. For the 'biography' that was Mithras's holy book . . . failed to persuade its readers that he had ever really appeared on earth to provide help for human beings . . .

Besides, Mithraism had no place for women; and it is they, as the cults of Isis and Cybele and Jesus made clear, who provided the largest numerical support for successful faiths.[12]

Jupiter of Doliche (in Commagene) was also revered. And Septimius, as we saw, honoured Hercules and Bacchus in their African guise (Chapter 11).[13] Elagabalus, young and contentious, overdid the tendency by enthusiastically importing to Rome all the paraphernalia of the Emesene cult of El-Gabal, with preposterous exaggerations which even found their way onto official coins (Plate 17), and did not, apparently, upset the Roman people, who enjoyed the entertainments involved, although the senate was not so happy.

Egyptian deities, too, were very popular. As we have seen, Septimius took on the hair-style of Serapis.[14] It has also been described how Caracalla, who likewise loved the god, built a temple for him, as well as a temple of Isis near the Colosseum. Isis, to whom he was as devoted as he was to Serapis, also appeared on his coins, celebrating his visit to Egypt in 215. Her cult aroused profound emotion. Conversely, a Capitoline Roman-style cult of Isis emerged in Egypt, in the time of Caracalla.

But it was the worship of the Sun, as we saw, which was truly pre-eminent at the period. There was a good deal of precedent for this. A figure of Sol had the features of Commodus, whose father Marcus Aurelius, on his death-bed, declared him to be the Rising Sun. A relief from Ephesus shows the deified Marcus ascending to the sky in the god's chariot which returns dead souls to their heavenly element. And it was the family of the Aurelii, from which Septimius untruthfully announced his descent, that had traditionally been charged with Sol's Roman cult. The Sun is called the Discoverer of Light, and his characteristic title 'Unconquerable' (INVICTVS) at this time finds increasing expression, and is applied directly to emperors who were linked with his worship.

Under Septimius and his family the solar cult almost took charge of the entire pantheon. His building the Septizodium or Septizonium seems to have displayed the emperor as Sun-god with seven planets around him, the seven spheres of which the Sun was Lord (Chapter 11). In this building the emperor acted as judge (cf. Chapter 9), just as his Parthian contemporaries dispensed justice in another star-studded hall. Septimius's politically powerful wife Julia Domna and her sister Julia Maesa were daughters of the high priest at the Syrian Sun-temple of Emesa. And Domna was the patron of Philostratus, who gave a pronouncedly solar emphasis to his Life of the sorcerer Apollonius of Tyana (see above). In this atmosphere, it was scarcely surprising that designs on imperial coinage show divergences from their customary Roman conservatism (Plate 8).

When Geta's brother Caracalla became ruler, the emphasis on Sun-worship became even stronger. Caracalla claimed, not entirely in jest, that he used the god's method of chariot-driving. A lion on his coinage indicates the derivation of his régime from Sol, and a little bronze portrait in the form of a shield endows him with its rays.

Then Elagabalus, as we have seen, though he adopted the names of Marcus Aurelius Antoninus which Caracalla had used before him, swept aside any caution or tradition in his haste to incorporate his own version of Sun-worship into the Roman imperial theology.[15] For this Roi Soleil imported his native, eastern local solar cult, unmodified – in the form of a black, phallic meteorite – into the centre and headship of the religion of Rome.

A huge temple was now built for this Sun-god at Rome (Chapter 10). And the deity's Semitic name ELAGAB(alus) or Baal, identified with Sol, strikes an outlandish note amid the traditions of the official coinage (Plate 17).

In keeping, however, with an age which was beginning to call its rulers the comrades of divinities rather than actual divinities themselves, the emperor Elagabalus does not himself claim identification with the god, preferring to recall his hereditary position as priest of the cult.

> He placed the Sun-god in a chariot adorned with gold and jewels and brought him out from the city to the suburbs. A six-horse chariot bore the Sun-god, the horses huge and flaw-lessly white, with expensive gold fittings and rich ornaments. No one held the reins, and no one rode in the chariot. The vehicle was escorted as if the Sun-god himself were the charioteer.

Elagabalus ran backwards in front of the chariot, facing the god and holding the horses' reins. He made the whole journey in this reverse fashion, looking up into the face of his god. Since he was unable to see where he was going, his route was paved with gold dust to keep him from stumbling and falling. And bodyguards supported him on each side to protect him from injury.

The people ran parallel to him, carrying torches and tossing wreaths and flowers. The statues of all the gods, the costly or sacred offerings in the temples, the imperial ornaments, and valuable heirlooms were carried by the cavalry and the entire praetorian guard in honour of the Sun-god.[16]

Elagabalus behaved too rashly, and was murdered. And yet in spite of this setback, the worship of the Sun did not cease to flourish and increase. The new emperor Severus Alexander, cousin to Elagabalus, repeatedly shows Sol on his coinage. But the god is now portrayed in classic form without Elagabalus's eastern exaggerations.

Probably Septimius's alleged anti-Jewish (and anti-Christian) edict in Egypt is fictitious.[17] But the Jews did not have a very easy time in his reign, as is illustrated by their rebellion, with the Samaritans, after the defeat of Niger.[18] Yet the Jews possessed their synagogues – at Dura-Europus the building seems to date from c. 235. And, before that, they had been led by a very distinguished rabbi, Judah I the Prince (135–217).

There were spasmodic persecutions of the Christians under Septimius, notably in Africa, starting in c. 200, and giving rise to the *Passion of Perpetua* (202–3). But although the emperor no doubt objected to the Christians' uncompromisingly lukewarm attitude to the state (and this lack of patriotic feeling is no doubt what caused the hostility they encountered at Byzantium during its siege), there is no evidence that Septimius, with his syncretistic views, initially took the lead in persecuting them, although he may have come, in due course, to do so. In any case, he showed no particular unwillingness or opposition when local authorities turned against the Christians. So Ulpian (Chapter 9) was able to put together a collection of anti-Christian edicts.

Yet Christianity, often inextricably associated with Sun-worship (see above), had come to stay.[19] And it was steadily increasing at a remarkable rate (unrecorded on the pagan imperial coinage), although the Christians were divided into warring factions:[20] notably, Hippolytus and Callistus (bishop of Rome) were at odds[21] and Numenius of Apamea in Syria earned Christian displeasure, because he was influenced by the dualistic, 'heretical' Gnostics (cf. also the dispute about the Montanists: see below). Nevertheless, the rise and recognition of Christianity is exemplified by the fact that Julia Mamaea knew and talked with both Hippolytus and Origen (Chapter 8). Moreover, there were churches at Edessa (*c.* 201) and Dura-Europus (*c.* 232–3), not to speak of the catacombs at Rome, of which the official organization by the Church started in *c.* 200.

Furthermore, Origen wrote well – better than any pagan of the period, except perhaps Longus. And so did Tertullian, and, to a lesser extent, Irenaeus and Clement of Alexandria, who were both earlier.

Irenaeus (*c.* 130–*c.* 202) was born in Asia Minor. But he spent most of his career in Gaul, where he became bishop of Lugdunum (Lyon) in *c.* 178, in which capacity he helped the 'heretics' known as Montanists, an austere, prophetic, ecstatic, apocalyptic movement among the Christians of Asia Minor, which was strongly opposed by the bishops. He wrote extensively (for the most part before the time of Septimius Severus). But just two of his works are still extant, the lengthy book *Adversus Haereses*, directed against the 'heretical' Gnostics (for the most part only available in a Latin translation of his original Greek), and the brief *Demonstration of Apostolic Preaching* (now only extant in an Armenian translation).

Irenaeus was at pains to emphasize that a great deal of Christianity was traditional. He is the principal surviving witness of a period in which the Church increasingly had to assert its claims against a variety of schismatic, 'heretical' bodies, although he himself (despite his writings) appealed to Victor, the bishop of Rome, in favour of toleration. Irenaeus displayed a keen expectation of Christ's Second Coming, and of God's millennial future kingdom upon earth.

Clement of Alexandria, born in *c.* 150 – probably at Athens – of pagan parentage, became a convert to Christianity, and after widespread travels studied under Pantaenus, director of the Catechetical Christian School at Alexandria, whom Clement warmly praised for his fidelity to the apostolic tradition. At that epoch, the Alexandrian School existed unofficially with the aim of teaching converts. Clement became ordained as a priest, and succeeded Pantaenus as director of the School some time before 200. But then in *c.* 202, when persecution broke out, he left Alexandria and took refuge elsewhere, dying between 211 and 216, perhaps in Asia Minor.

Many of Clement's writings are lost. But the *Tutor* (*c.* 190–5) is almost completely extant. Its purpose is to outline the ethical teaching of Jesus Christ. And then came the eight books of his *Miscellanies* (*c.* 200–2), concerned, for the most part, with the superiority of Christian philosophical ideas over those of the pagans, since Clement, like Irenaeus, was eager to resist the charge that Christianity meant an abandonment of ancestral customs. However, *Quis Dives Salvetur?* urges an un-pagan non-attachment to worldly possessions.

Clement, although serene and optimistic, underwent a good deal of criticism. This was partly because of his extensive knowledge of Greek literature, since he was said to have introduced too much Hellenism and humanism into his Christianity.[22] Yet his writings mark an epoch in early Christian intellectual development. Above all, Clement was convinced that his faith could be reconciled with reason and philosophy. But he is one of the fathers of monastic spiritualism as well.

Tertullian (Quintus Septimius Florens Tertullianus, *c.* 160–240) was born in or near Carthage. Thirty-one of his works are still extant. He was given a legal training, and took an early interest in Stoicism. But pagan morality, or lack of it, displeased him. And this displeasure, combined with an admiration for the Christian martyrs who had died for their faith, drove him into adopting a puritanical Christian position (*c.* 195), which he justified at Carthage with the assistance of all his legal and rhetorical talents – including a marked capacity for irony. In *c.* 197 Tertullian composed *Ad Martyras, Ad Nationes* and the *Apologeticus* in order to defend Christianity, and martyrdom in its cause, against the popular belief that Christians were atheists addicted to black magic. Then, during the next seven years, he wrote a number of pieces concentrating on the ethical problems raised by his faith: for which he showed an austere enthusiasm, declaring war against the rest of the world.

In *c.* 203, puritanical as he was, Tertullian was converted to the severe doctrine of Montanism (cf. above on Irenaeus). By *c.* 207 he had come to take up an extreme and virulent position, attacking, in various works, all forms of what he called 'idolatry'. He argued strongly against a tactful or compromising approach to authority, and indeed, against the whole tradition of the Roman imperial government. In 212 he addressed an open letter to the governor of Africa, Scapula, in which he made an eloquent plea for religious freedom and non-interference, requesting a cessation of what had become the government's policy of harassing the Christians.

In his latest surviving work, *De Pudicitia* (*On Modesty* or *Chastity*), he urged the bishop of Rome, Callistus (217–22), against any form of moderation or relaxation. And he himself abandoned Montanism in order to establish his own Tertullianist sect, which was even more rigorous.

Unlike other Christian writers of this period, Tertullian wrote in Latin, giving this branch of Christian literature a splendid start. He has been described as the first Latin churchman.[23] And he was, undoubtedly, one of the creators of western Christian thinking as well.[24]

Origen (Origenes Adamantius) was born in Alexandria of Christian parents, probably in 185 or 186, and died in 254 or 255. He was an Egyptian who wrote in Greek. We know about him from the Greek historian Eusebius (c. AD 260–340). Origen was educated by his father Leonides, who was one of those who died in the persecution of 202, during the reign of Septimius Severus. In the following year Origen became head of the Alexandrian Catechetical School (mentioned above), in which he had attended lectures. So as to obtain a better understanding of pagan habits of thought, he also went to the lectures of the esoteric Neo-Platonist Ammonius Saccas at Alexandria. Origen's work there as a teacher, however, was broken off by Caracalla's massacre in the city (215). He then moved to Rome, where he voluntarily underwent castration. Subsequently he travelled widely, and was ordained as a priest in Greece (c. 231), though Alexandria remained his base, at least in his own thoughts.

Yet despite his fame, the adventurous nature of his theories meant that his relations with Demetrius, the Christian bishop of Alexandria, were poor, and he was exiled from the place and deposed from his priestly post (232). However, the deposition was ignored in Judaea. Origen established himself at Caesarea Maritima, where he went on with his work, and attracted many pupils. (But in the persecution of Trajanus Decius (249–50) he suffered tortures; and he died at Tyre.)

Origen's writings were voluminous, and their range wide, though only a small proportion of what he wrote has survived. He composed a great vindication of Christianity (*Against Celsus*) late in his life. But earlier he had been a pioneer in the textual criticism and exegesis of the Bible, and in systematic theology. His works include the *De Principiis*, an exposition of Christian doctrine written before he left

Alexandria, the *De Oratione* (*c.* 231), about various aspects of prayer, and his main life-work, the critical *Hexapla* (begun before 231, but not finished for another thirteen years), in which the Hebrew and various Greek texts of the Old Testament were set side by side.

Origen was said to have been sent an escort of soldiers by Julia Domna (Chapter 8) in 217, so that she could hear him preach. He also preached, it was reported, to Julia Mamaea. Like Longus, he was one of the most prolific writers of antiquity. And he proved to be the most influential theologian of the early Greek Christian Church, though he has been described as world-denying and even illiberal.[25] Origen was utterly opposed to the secular, pagan state, which was, indeed, doomed to fall to the Christians. For, with such eloquence behind it, Christianity's expansion continued apace.[26]

EPILOGUE

Edward Gibbon had this to say about Septimius Severus: 'Posterity, who experienced the fatal effects of his maxims and example, justly considered him as the principal author of the decline of the Roman empire.'[1] Septimius died in 211, and those who professed to belong to his dynasty lived on until 235. Yet the western Roman empire did not finally fall until 476. That was a long time after Septimius's death. How far, then, is Gibbon's verdict justified?

That long period of time, between 235 and 476, operates against its justification. A great many things happened in the intervening centuries. And it is too acrobatic a feat to detect the origins of collapse so far back. Roughly speaking, what happened was that the empire fell apart after the Severans, was forcibly brought together again as a single unit, and underwent formal division, and only thereafter did the western empire decline and fall in 476. The eastern (Byzantine) empire, on the other hand, continued to exist, with one interruption, until 1453.

Yet Septimius, and his somewhat insignificant successors, did do certain things which undermined the strength of the Roman world. First, they encouraged autocracy. Woe betide anyone who contradicted Septimius to his face. He was a lord and a god (*dominus et deus*) more than a *princeps*. And Elagabalus may have been the emperor who insisted that everyone should grovel in his presence, performing an *adoratio*, perhaps partly as a precaution against assassination attempts. We also learn that, in the time of Severus Alexander, members of the imperial Council remained standing in the emperor's presence. But all those are outward trivialities, although at the same time they are signs of how things had come to be. The emperor was supreme autocrat, to an extent that had never been seen before.

Equally serious, as Gibbon recognizes, was the total authority that had been gained by the army. The soldiers ruled the empire on behalf of the emperors, who would not, or, more probably, could not, do anything to halt or mitigate this process. It was a far cry from the careful balance of powers – including prominence of the senate – devised by Augustus, however much these later monarchs might invoke his name.

The only refuge, apart from novels and the law, was religion. And here, too, Gibbon apportions blame. He sees the Christians as one of the forces that brought down the empire. It would hardly be reasonable, however, to blame the Severans for this, or indeed for the rise of Christianity, which, it is true, they only ineffectively tried to curb and prevent. Here the army was of no help at all, because although almost entirely pagan (Mithraism was its favourite cult), we never hear of any serious military attempt to exalt paganism against the rise of Christianity.

But the most serious threat to the empire was external. And this only became evident in the very last few of the years that are the subject of this book. The threat was then provided, jointly, by the Germans north of the Danube and east of the Rhine, and by the Persians who had become the far more formidable successors of the Parthians in Mesopotamia and Iran. One of the reasons why the Parthians succumbed to the Persians was because Septimius Severus had dealt them such severe blows. Yet it is doubtful if he can be held responsible for the fact that they afterwards collapsed and were succeeded by the much more dangerous Persians. Nevertheless, the result was, at the end of our period, that Rome was confronted by this perilous menace to the east as well as by the new and equally dangerous confederation of the Alamanni (Germans) in the north and east – a danger which, as we have seen, Dio Cassius, for example, does not realize (any more than he foresees the later Christian supremacy).

So perhaps it was just as well that the Roman rulers of the epoch did everything they could to strengthen the army. For the soldiers were needed. And Septimius Severus emerges as the author of measures which allowed the empire to survive for another quarter of a century before its first serious collapse. In particular, Septimius somehow managed, despite all his expenditure, to leave the state, at the time of his death, much better off than he had found it when he came to the throne. His successors were, no doubt, inadequate. But they could not wholly undo all that Septimius had done to shore up the empire, notably by this financial miracle.

APPENDIX
The literary sources

The surviving literary sources which ought to help us to build up a history of the period are pretty poor, especially if we compare them with earlier historians. (And we are not helped by the fact that those novelists who wrote well (Chapter 10) went to such trouble to avoid topicality and conceal their dates.) As a result, these literary sources are virtually useless to the historian; except, to a limited extent, Dio Cassius, who lived during the period, and occupied a prominent place at Rome (he must be distinguished from Dio Chrysostom of Prusa (Brusa), AD 40–after 112).

Dio Cassius (Cassius Dio Cocceianus), the son of Cassius Apronianus, who held the governorships of Cilicia and Dalmatia, was born in about AD 163 at Nicaea (Iznik). Dio came to Rome in the opening years of the principate of Commodus, and entered the senate while the latter was still alive and on the throne. In 193, during the brief reign of Pertinax, Dio was nominated to a praetorship, which he occupied during the following year, after the elevation to the throne of Septimius Severus. In 205 or 206, he became consul, and under the régime of Severus Alexander he served successively as governor of Africa, Dalmatia and Upper Pannonia. In 229 Dio received the honour of a second consulship, in which his colleague was Severus Alexander himself. On the latter's suggestion, however, Dio moved away from the city, where his rigorous discipline had made him unpopular with the praetorian guardsmen.

Dio compiled a *Roman History* in eighty books, of which nineteen have survived complete, sixteen in abbreviated form, and three in part. Epitomes and summaries of missing portions are also available.

He aimed conscientiously at an accurate and systematic reconstruction and synthesis. But, in this, he was not entirely successful. At least, however, his work enlarges our awareness of the bicultural nature of the Roman empire, illustrating the renaissance of the Greek cities. Dio's version of Roman history is valuable in one other respect too, because it is based on personal participation at a high level over a more prolonged period than any other ancient historian could muster.

We are told that he presented Septimius Severus with a work written by himself and entitled *The History of the Civil Wars*. But then, his hopes for Septimius deceived, Dio does not abstain from criticizing him. He hates Caracalla. Next, he describes what a shock it was to have a mere knight on the throne (Macrinus). And he is outraged by the immoral behaviour of Elagabalus.[1] His 'Augustan' debate between Agrippa and Maecenas, though entirely unauthentic, displays Dio's desire that the senate should recover, if not its power, at least its prestige.

On the whole, he abstains from detailed description, which he regards as unworthy of the dignity of history. But the result is that his narrative generally lacks vividness, except when he indulges his taste for anecdotes. Dio employed a style that was archaic and sparely Attic. Yet he nevertheless laced his writings with rhetorical devices. And he occasionally indulged in dramatization. His professed models were Thucydides, who prompted his concentration on political themes, and the orator Demosthenes, who stimulated his taste for rhetorical elaboration. Dio probably had some link with his own contemporary Philostratus (Chapter 11).

He is usefully aware of the difficulty of obtaining accurate information about imperial history. But he failed to see the growth, and danger to the empire, either of the northern, German, danger or of Christianity.

He probably wrote his book in three stages, the first in 196/7 or 202, a second in *c.* 219, and later a third.

Herodian of Syria (early third century AD) compiled an eight-book history of the period from Marcus Aurelius to Gordian III (AD 180–238).

> Moralising and rhetorical, his work is superficial, although its value increases with his contemporary knowledge and information.
>
> He belonged to the educated class in a country where Aramaic was still the spoken language. . . . Herodian [was a] trilingual Syrian. . . .

It may be suggested that he joined the civil service after the defeat of Pescennius Niger by Septimius Severus.

His early association with the Syrian dynasty at Rome would account for the amazing 'Romanness' of his outlook. Herodian is so thoroughly patriotic . . . and so Romanized that he can speak of his fellow non-Romans as barbarians, and can offer an analysis of his fellow-Syrians that is thoroughly unflattering. . . .

Herodian offers a moralizing account of the downward spiral of the empire. We must credit Herodian with enough sense of history to recognise that the death of Marcus Aurelius signified the end of an era. Herodian's chief concern is with the corruption that accompanied the decline in Rome's world position.

That he was not a professional historian is apparent. . . . He is a rhetorician, pompous, repetitive and derivative. . . . His insight into causes and motivation is superficial and unconvincing. . . . Herodian's geography is vague, [his data] indefinite and inexact. His speeches are tedious and wearing. His belief that he was a stylist is misleading. And he is much less thorough than Dio Cassius [whom he read].[2]

Marius Maximus probably wrote under Severus Alexander. He was a biographer of the emperors from Nerva (AD 96–8) to Elagabalus, a 'continuer' and imitator of Suetonius. But his work is lost. The biographer who bears this name is probably the Marius Maximus who governed Syria, Africa and Asia, and was prefect of the city of Rome in AD 217.

He apparently had a taste for what was trivial, anecdotic and scandalous. And he is accused of verbosity and unreliability.

He was extensively used by the *Historia Augusta*, the title given by I. Casaubon (1603) to a collection of 'biographies' of Roman emperors, Caesars and usurpers from AD 117 to 284 (Hadrian to Carinus and Numerian). The work was allegedly composed by six persons in the epoch of Diocletian (284–305) and Constantine I the Great (306–37). But the whole of the *Historia Augusta* is permeated with fraudulence. And even its main professions (date, dedication and authorship) deserve no credence. Perhaps one man perpetrated the entire work. He was evidently writing in a later age, towards the end of the fourth century.[3]

The *Historia Augusta* displays pro-senatorial bias, and does not approve of hereditary monarchy – or of interference by the army. It offers a far too favourable picture of Severus Alexander, and in general its omissions and confusions are serious.

Syme sums up what can be said for and against the work.

> The *Historia Augusta* . . . is the only Latin source of any compass for a long tract in the annals of Imperial Rome. . . .
>
> The work is not a 'forgery' but an 'imposture' or 'impersonation'.[4]

A section of the *Life of Elagabalus* is the best part of the *Historia Augusta*. The work cites Marius Maximus twenty-six times, three times by name. But he is, it appears, drastically abbreviated in the process. One of the total inventions of the work is the oratory of Clodius Albinus. The *Life of Macrinus*, too, has been described as diffuse, careless and cynical.

There was said to have been a pagan literary revival under Severus Alexander. But if so it produced very little that is worthwhile, except, probably, the novel of Longus, and some legal work. Other writers of the period occasionally throw a small amount of light on what happened.[5] And so do later authors.[6]

Inscriptions, coins and medallions are helpful.[7] For coins and medallions are very abundant indeed: Septimius issued 342 different coins in his first three years. But the point of view which they convey is not always sufficiently informative, because it is naturally that of the ruler and his house.

EMPERORS

Septimius Severus	AD 193–8
Septimius Severus and Caracalla	198–209
Septimius Severus, Caracalla and Geta	209–11
Caracalla and Geta	211–12
Caracalla	212–17
Macrinus	217–18
Macrinus and Diadumenian	218
Elagabalus	218–22
Severus Alexander	222–35

ABBREVIATIONS*

AB	A. Birley, *Septimius Severus: The African Emperor* (1971)
BMC	H. Mattingly, *Coins of the Roman Empire in the British Museum*, Vol. V (1950)
CAH	*Cambridge Ancient History*, Vol. XII (1939)
CIL	*Corpus Inscriptionum Latinarum*
JBWP	J. B. Ward-Perkins, *Roman Imperial Architecture* (1981)
JRS	*Journal of Roman Studies*
RDJ	R. Duncan-Jones, *Money and Government in the Roman Empire* (1994)
RIC	H. Mattingly and E. A. Sydenham, *Roman Imperial Coinage*, Vol. IV, Part 1 (1936)
RS/*EB*	R. Syme, *Emperors and Biography* (1971)
SHA	*Scriptores Historiae Augustae*

* References to Dio (Cassius) include references to the Epitomes of his work (cf. Appendix).

NOTES

1 It has been argued by some that the 'Antonine period' should be considered as having continued until AD 235 (RS/EB, p. 73). That was certainly the wish of the emperors during that epoch. But it seems more correct and helpful to regard the Severans, if we may use the term for the emperors from 193 to 235, as a separate entity, who came to the throne when the empire – which had been in a state of transition under the previous dynasty – had entered upon a new phase of its existence.

1 SEPTIMIUS SEVERUS AND THE STRUGGLE FOR POWER

1 There is some uncertainty about Septimius's forebears. It may have been his great-grandfather who was Punic, and came from Rome to become a knight. His father Publius Septimius Geta, shortly before his death, moved to Cirta (Constantine), where a memorial was erected to him. Pollienus Auspex, a senator who became governor of Lower Moesia, made a joke about the emperor's ancestry, which was probably not very well received. The emperor had two first cousins who rose high in the senate. He himself came to Rome before *c.* 173.

2 There has been much discussion about the extent of the *Africitas* of Septimius Severus. Was John Malalas, of Antioch, right about the colour of his skin (AB, p. 62)? Was he more dark-skinned than, say, most south Italians? T. D. Barnes, *Historia* XVI, p. 106, thinks that his *Africitas* has been overrated. Yet the patron of his house was Hercules, who had a powerful African guise (Chapters 5, 12).

3 Septimius may have been aware of the fate of Pertinax by 1 April (for the suggestion that he foresaw, or knew about it in advance, cf. AB, p. 155). He addressed a meeting of self-proclamation on 13 April 193.

4 For his 'legionary coinage', honouring the legions that supported him, cf. *BMC*, pp. lxxxiif., 21ff. All the Rhine and Danube legions are mentioned except Legio X Gemina, which may have done something to incur Septimius's displeasure; *ibid.*, p. lxxxii.

5 The fact that Pertinax refused to allow his own son to accept the title of Caesar lends some weight to that suggestion. Septimius took the name Pertinax, whom, whatever information he may have possessed about his forthcoming fall (see n. 3 above), he admired for his frugality (*SHA, Septimius* 22), and for his claim to continue the traditions of Marcus Aurelius; although it is uncertain whether he took the name of his own free will or under pressure. Perhaps the former, because he intended to pose as the deceased emperor's avenger. But the memory of Pertinax was not very popular with the army, and Septimius virtually dropped the name in *c.* 198, or soon afterwards.

6 But very little credence should be attached to the account of his parentage and ancestry in *SHA, Pescennius Niger* 3; cf. RS/*EB*, p. 7.

7 *SHA, Pescennius Niger* 10 (discipline). 'Neither good nor bad', Dio 75.6.

8 Nicaea (Iznik), which supported Pescennius Niger, was seriously at odds with Nicomedia (Izmit), which did not: Herodian 3.2.9.

9 The date of this battle of Issus is uncertain. It has been variously attributed to the end of 193, to early summer 194, or to some period a year or two later.

10 On the mintages of Pescennius I received a letter of 28 March 1995 from Professor T. V. Buttrey, adding to his comments in *Numismatic Chronicle* (1992), pp. vi–xxii; cf. R. Bland, A. Burnett and S. Bendall, *Numismatic Chronicle* (1987), pp. 65–83. At Antioch, tetradrachms issued in his name include the inscription ΠPONOIA ΘEΩN (*Providentia Deorum*). It would be useful, however, to know more about S.C. and P.P. on some of Pescennius's coins, where they appear in surprising contexts.

11 AB, pp. 185, 188, n. 1. Septimius alleged that Clodius Albinus had been behind the murder of Pertinax.

12 There are various accounts of Clodius Albinus's character (*SHA, Albinus* 10.1–4). Once again, however, we cannot recover the truth, since he lost the war and what we have is largely his enemy's attitude. But we should view the *Historia Augusta*'s account of his writings with grave suspicion (cf. Appendix). It is also more than doubtful that there were as many as 150,000 soldiers on either side at the battle of Lugdunum (Lyon).

13 It is conceivable that Septimius even 'adopted' Clodius Albinus as his son, but this cannot be regarded as certain (or even, perhaps, likely).

14 But the names of those executed, in *SHA, Septimius* 13, must be regarded as partly or largely fictitious.

15 Dio 76.8.

16 *SHA, Septimius* 1.4 reports a tradition that in his youth he rebelled against the literary influence of Marcus Cornelius Fronto (M. Grant, *The Antonines* (London, 1994), pp. 84ff.).

2 THE PRAETORIANS AND THEIR PREFECTS: PLAUTIANUS

1 Herodian 1.13.1ff. But this looks rather like an official explanation, and we do not know how, in fact, the dismissal of the praetorians was done. Cf. discussion in AB, p. 165 and n. 1.

2 The praetorian guardsmen were said to have received at least 150 million

sestertii from Didius Julianus, though there was apparently some measure of dissatisfaction.

3 It is not quite certain that this was the *immediate* arrangement. But it is probable. The city cohorts (under their prefect, the *praefectus urbi*) were also increased in size, and the number of *vigiles* (fire brigade and occasional police force) doubled.

4 Herodian 4.4.7.

5 Dio 80.18. The praetorian guardsmen disliked Elagabalus's promotion of his favourites (notably Comazon Eutychianus, who became praetorian prefect).

6 Though our sources sometimes make it difficult to distinguish between the praetorian guard and the legions.

7 Plautianus, a Fulvius, was said (probably correctly) to be related to the mother of Septimius Severus, Fulvia Pia.

8 The story (later spread around) that Plautianus plotted against Septimius need not necessarily be believed.

9 Dio 76.15.

10 CONCORDIAE AETERNAE on her coins (*BMC*, pp. 235–400f.) was an untruth, or wishful thinking. PROPAGO IMPERI also appears (*ibid.*, pp. 406ff.). But we know nothing of any children.

11 The Arcus Argentariorum (Arch of the Bankers) at Rome (Chapter 11) is a noteworthy example.

3 THE GESTURES OF SEPTIMIUS

1 There were temples of the House of the Severi, for example, at Cuicul (Djemila), JBWP, p. 196, fig. 293: cf. Chapter 5, n. 3 and caption to Plate 32.

2 The deification of Commodus, however much it annoyed the senate (and there may have been an element of imperial deliberateness and malice in this), would have pleased the army, who were the first to be told the news.

3 *CIL*, VIII.9317.

4 Caracalla may have been given the name Antoninus on the capture of Ctesiphon (Chapter 5). The name appears on the coins of Alexandria before 28 August 196. There is a head of the young Caracalla at Hanover: F. Abbate, *Roman Art* (London, 1972), p. 102, plate 66.

5 *SHA, Diadumenianus* VI, cf. *Septimius* 10.3–6, *Caracalla* 3.2.

6 DESTINATO IMPERAT., *BMC*, pp. xlv, 52. The decision was echoed throughout the empire, for example on the Arch at Lepcis Magna, Chapter 11. 'Caesar' also occurs on early rescripts. One object of these moves was to curb the intentions and claims of Septimius's brother, Publius Septimius Geta, *SHA, Septimius* 10.

7 But a diagnosis of Caracalla's ailment is impossible – except that he was believed to be impotent. At one time he was thought to have imported syphilis from the east. At any rate, his coins refer to his interest in Aesculapius, *BMC*, p. 451 etc.

8 Faustina the younger and Pertinax were also said to suffer from gout.

9 Geta looked like his father, and that gave him a certain popularity. Coins

with AETERNIT. IMPERI have three busts, of Septimius, Caracalla and Geta, *RIC*, p. 77, no. 697, and H. Mattingly, *BMC*, pp. cxxviii, cxxxv, cxliv, cxlviii, 191 etc. A red jasper from Castlesteads shows Septimius as Serapis and his two sons as the Dioscuri. Septimius spent two years in Campania, partly, it was believed, in order to distract his sons from the pleasures of the city. But when he took both Caracalla and Geta to Britain (Herodian 3.10.3, 4.13.3–6, Chapter 5), he left the latter in the British province so that he could gain experience of administration.

10 PERPETVA CONCORDIA, *BMC*, pp. xlv, 360, was the reverse of the truth, particularly after the fall of Plautianus. For Septimius's late (?) recognition of this, see Dio 76.14.1–7, 17.5.

4 THE SUCCESSORS

1 There were some doubts, however, whether Julia Domna was really the mother of Caracalla rather than Septimius's first wife, Paccia Marciana (Chapter 1). But probably Julia Domna was his mother.

2 Dio 77.1.3. The mint no doubt tried to forget that it had issued types of Janus (or Jupiter Biceps?). This was presumably to symbolize the duality of the empire (*BMC* pp. clxxxviii, 422) – although an earlier appearance of Janus, under Pertinax, had merely referred to his accession on the first day of the year (*ibid.*, p. xxxix).

3 Dio 79.6. For Lunus, whom Caracalla was going to revere when he was killed, cf. *SHA, Caracalla* 6.7.23–5, Herodian 4.13.3. Or was it Selene (the Moon)?

4 M. Grant, *The Roman Emperors* (London, 1985), pp. 223f.

5 Macrinus's friends found the war very burdensome: Dio 79.11.

6 LIBERALITAS AVG., *RIC*, p. 84, no. 730, *BMC*, p. 506; but cf. p. ccxxv, Macrinus's 'honours to the dead man's memory'.

7 And Macrinus annoyed the western legionaries by recruiting on a large scale, exclusively in Syria.

8 Macrinus's enemies rudely called Diadumenianus 'pseudo-Antoninus'.

9 Dio 78.9.2, *SHA, Caracalla* 11.5.

10 The version 'Heliogabalus' has no contemporary support.

11 *SHA, Macrinus* 9.4. But the claim was not very impressive, because Caracalla was supposedly impotent (cf. Chapter 3, n. 7).

12 Is that the point of INDVLGENTIA on coins in Severus Alexander's name under Elagabalus (*BMC*, p. 571, nos 264f.)?

13 Herodian 5.17.8.

14 Caracalla, as high priest (*pontifex maximus*) (like Domitian, AD 81–96), had punished a Vestal Virgin guilty of incest. There exists the upper part of the statue of a Vestal, A. W. Lawrence, *Classical Sculpture*, p. 379 and plate 143b. The Temple and House of the Vestals in their present form date from the Severan period.

15 *RIC*, pp. 87f., *BMC*, p. xliii.

16 Julian, *Caesars*, p. 313A. For Severus Alexander's head at Schloss Fasanerie (and other portraits) see Chapter 11, and cf. Plate 22.

17 *SHA, Severus Alexander* 44.2.

5 THE PROVINCES AND ITALY: THE *CONSTITUTIO ANTONINIANA*

1 Cf. ROMAE AETERNAE on coins; see below, in Chapter 11, n. 27.

2 For the stationing of a legion at Albanum (Albano), see Chapter 6. It is doubtful whether Septimius was completely in sympathy with, or fully understood, Italian pride and tradition (Chapter 1).

3 It has been remarked that the accession of Septimius was a symptom, not a cause, of the rise of Africa, which had already been prosperous before. Yet certainly there was a great deal of building in north Africa under Septimius (Chapter 11). And the patron of his house was the Hercules of Africa (Chapter 12), from which he came. The meaning of the coin inscription INDVLGENTIA AVGG. IN CARTH(aginem) (*BMC*, index V) remains uncertain. But probably it refers to some improvement of the water supply at Carthage, *RIC*, p. 78, no. 702. Most regular troops in Africa could now be replaced by *numeri* (native militias) (Chapter 6). The reign of Septimius also represents the high-water mark of African participation in the higher administration at Rome. There was also a Temple of the Severan Family at Cuicul (Djemila).

4 Septimius's early visit to Syria (Chapter 1) had a great influence on him. Ulpian was generous to Tyre, which hated Berytus (Beirut). And the Laodiceans hated Antioch, where Septimius inaugurated his second consulship (with Caracalla). The Syrian coinages of Septimius need further attention.

5 *Municipia* were promoted into colonies at Carnuntum (Petronell) and Aquincum (Budapest). New and improved *emporia* were organized in Thrace.

6 For Septimius as *propagator imperii* see AB, pp. 17, 184, n. 1, 264.

7 A stone fort was built at Salzburg early in the third century AD. And there were advanced earthen mounds in Germany, with walls.

8 J. N. Adams, *JRS* 84 (1994), p. 37: a detachment of the Legio III Augusta arrived there on 24 January 201. Septimius probably visited the new frontier works at Lambaesis (Tazzoult). The north African frontier was generally improved.

9 Septimius had to contend with King Vologases V (IV) of Parthia (*c.* 192–*c.* 207), whom at first, it was said, he handled with discretion, declining the name 'Parthicus' so as not to hurt the king's feelings, and suggesting that he himself was only fighting against Parthia's allies, not against Parthia itself. Before the end of 195 he handed back Osrhoene (Edessa) to King Abgar VIII (or IX), as a client enclosure within the province of Mesopotamia. Abgar adopted the name of Septimius, and later went to Rome. But the Parthians occupied Osrhoene, and were expelled from it and from Adiabene (197), and it was perhaps in December of that year that the Parthian city of Ctesiphon was taken. For surviving reliefs of Ardashir I, cf. J. M. C. Toynbee, *Roman Historical Portraits* (London, 1978), pp. 172–5. Dura-Europus became an important garrison town: cf. JBWP, pp. 350ff.

10 Septimius, an indefatigable sightseer, entered Egypt before 30 August 199.

11 Ulpian (Chapter 9), *Digest* 32A.
12 It was probably after the defeat of Clodius Albinus that Roman Britain was divided into two provinces, Britannia Superior (with legions at Deva (Chester) and Isca Silurum (Caerleon) and Inferior (with garrison at Eburacum (York)). Cf. Syria, also divided into two (Coele and Phoenice), probably in 193–5: S. N. Miller, *CAH*, pp. 11, 27.
13 Dio 76.13.1: cf. 70.12.5, 22.13.
14 *SHA, Septimius* 18.2. Did Septimius ever cross the River Bodotria (Firth of Forth)? Does TRAIECTVS on coins (*BMC*, pp. 353, 390 (AD 208)) refer to this (C. W. C. Oman, *Numismatic Chronicle* (1931), pp. 137ff.)? But the bridge seems too elaborate for a mere campaign structure: *RIC*, p. 80, no. 709.
15 Herodian 3.14.1
16 For Carpow, with its turf rampart, stone gates, stone principal buildings and timber barrack-blocks, cf. AB, pp. 17, 258, 270.
17 The *Constitutio Antoniniana* is not even mentioned on the coinage, unless LIBERTAS is an indirect reference to it. Alone of the jurists (Chapter 9), Ulpian alludes to it (*Digest* I, 5, 17). One of the reasons why it may not have seemed very sweeping at the time was because the army had so greatly increased the number of citizens. A. d'Ors Perez-Peix wrote five or six articles on the subject. Cf. *RDJ*, p. 16.
18 Cf. Dio 78.9: minimized by some moderns, perhaps wrongly.
19 This meant that it was by no means true that 'the law is no respecter of persons'.
20 The Parthians had attempted to postpone the evil day of their collapse by grants of provincial autonomy.
21 Forts and perhaps other buildings continued to be constructed in north Britain: see next chapter.
22 For subsidies at this period, see *RDJ*, pp. 44f.

6 THE ARMY: THE MILITARY MONARCHY

1 Cf. now R. Alston, *JRS* 84 (1994), p. 115.
2 The hatred of the soldiers for the bourgeoisie has probably been over-stressed; though it could, at times, be discerned.
3 Service as a soldier assisted a man's passage to the centurionate.
4 But in order that the legions should not become *too* strong, it was arranged that their commanders must never be the legionaries' compatriots. (Here the troops in Syria were perhaps also in mind, since they reached their peak during this period.) There were to be twenty-four legions in pairs, distributed round twelve provinces out of thirty-two. German and Spanish bodyguards for the emperors were revived; Caracalla was accused of preferring barbarians (Chapter 5).
5 E. Gibbon, *The Decline and Fall of the Roman Empire*, Chapter 5 (Everyman edn, p. 140).
6 Dio 78.3.2.
7 Dio 79.36.
8 For British roads, see S. N. Miller, *CAH*, p. 32, nn. 2–3.

7 FINANCE

1 C. J. Bullock, *Politics, Finance and Consequences* (Cambridge, Mass., 1939), pp. 3f. James Wilson was the first of British India's Finance Ministers.

2 At Ephesus (Selçuk), the price of a loaf had doubled in a hundred years. But for our general lack of information about inflation rates cf. *RDJ*, p. 16.

3 Dio 80.3 complains of the expense of the Parthian wars – which was partly (though surely not wholly) offset by the loot captured during them.

4 Cf. ANNONA on coins, in more general terms: *BMC*, index V; AD 197–8 etc.

5 This was the grim task of the city councils, and their steering committees. See also n. 8 below. For the collection of revenue in kind in the under-monetized empire see *RDJ*, p. 3.

6 Oil was sent for from Africa.

7 LAETITIA TEMPORVM (*BMC*, index II; AD 201–6) makes the most of all this. The type had appeared under Pertinax. For the *congiaria* of Septimius, cf. *RDJ*, p. 10.

8 The taxes were farmed to corporations, which helped the government. See also n. 5 above. For the probability of heavier taxes under Septimius, cf. *RDJ*, pp. 15, 56. For Egypt as the only province which provides much evidence about taxation, see *ibid.*, p. 47.

9 A special body under imperial control, the *res privata principis*, was set up (or, more probably, developed from smaller origins) to receive these properties and funds. It had a branch of counterpart in Gaul, to deal with the confiscated properties of those who had supported Clodius Albinus. For the enormous fiscal proceeds from all the executions cf. *RDJ*, p. 6.

10 This created difficulties in the raising of taxes. Illicit exchange rates flourished. For the chronology of debasements at this period, cf. *RDJ*, p. 101, and for the gold–silver ratio *ibid.*, p. 218.

11 The relation of the *antoninianus* to the *denarius* does not seem to have been satisfactorily adjusted, unless the market discount of the *denarius* was now recognized, at thirty-six to the *aureus*. The debased and unstable *denarius*, along with the *antoninianus*, was used to pay the troops.

12 *Tres Monetae* (*BMC*, index III), Aeqvitas (*BMC*, index V).

13 Caracalla also issued a double *aureus*.

14 *SHA, Macrinus* 9.5. For the complaints against Macrinus, see Dio 78.12.7, *RDJ*, p. 10.

15 R. A. G. Carson, *Principal Coins of the Romans*, Vol II (31 BC–AD 296) (London 1980), p. 88, no. 731. Rebuilding of mint? Restoration of *denarius*? The abrupt discontinuation of the *antoninianus* caused an increase in the production of *denarii*, to meet the demands of military pay. For the continued deterioration of the weight of the *aureus*, cf. *RDJ*, p. 216; and for the *congiaria* of Elagabalus and Severus Alexander *ibid.*, p. 90.

16 *SHA, Severus Alexander* 32.5, etc. For the sale of the palace dwarfs, see *RDJ*, p. 10.

8 THE SYRIAN WOMEN

1 We had better avoid the term 'oriental', which sounds pejorative nowadays.

2 Philostratus, *Apollonius of Tyana* 13: the 'rhetorical exercises'; G. R. S. Mead, *Apollonius of Tyana: The Philosopher-Reformer of the First Century AD*, ed. L. Shephard (New York, 1966), pp. 53, 55: the 'salon'.

3 A sardonyx cameo in the British Museum shows Julia Domna as Luna (Selene, the Moon).

4 *BMC*, pp. xiii, 122, 124, etc. FELICITAS SAECVLI: four busts, including Julia Domna's: *RIC*, p. 77, nos 69f.

5 'Varius' (the name of Julia Soaemias's husband, Sextus Varius Marcellus of Apamea (Qalaat-al-Mudik)), was probably derived from an Arabic word for moon, and 'Soaemias' from the Arabic 'Suheina', 'Little Arrow'.

6 There had apparently already been a small issue of coins for Julia Mamaea during the reign of Elagabalus: *BMC*, pp. 571, 614.

7 *SHA*, *Severus Alexander* 3.11; cf. S. Perowne, *The Caesars' Wives* (London, 1974), p. 169.

8 J. P. C. Kent and M. and A. Hirmer, *Roman Coins* (London, 1978), plate 120, fig. 420.

9 THE LAWYERS

1 AB, p. 238, n. 1 (on *SHA*, *Caracalla* 83.3).

2 But Papinian's relationship, if any, to Septimius Severus and Julia Domna is uncertain.

3 Dio 77.10.7, 14.6.

4 The emperor's edicts went back to Republican *edicta magistratuum*, especially of praetors and curule aediles (whose duties included the supervision of the market-place. In the provinces quaestors did this). Cf. also Ulpian, who likewise wrote on *The Edict*.

5 Ulpian, *Digest* I, 3, 41. Imperial *constitutiones* had acquired legal validity, according to Ulpian, *Digest* I, 4, 1, pr.-1.

6 The 'laws of citation', of the fourth and fifth centuries (W. Kunkel, *An Introduction to Roman Legal and Constitutional History* (Oxford, 1966), pp. 145ff.), give special prominence to the views expressed by five jurists.

10 THE NOVEL: LONGUS

1 M. Grant, *Greeks and Romans: A Social History* (London 1992), pp. 1f. The prolific writer Galen, the doctor (on whom I am preparing a book) lived on into the reign of Septimius Severus, but had written most of his works earlier.

2 P. Turner (trans.), *Longus: Daphnis and Chloe* (Harmondsworth, 1968), pp. 9ff.

3 But the date of the 'classic' *Aethiopica* of Heliodorus of Emesa remains much disputed: N. Holzberg, *The Ancient Novel: An Introduction* (London, 1995), p. 104, T. Hägg, *The Novel in Antiquity* (University of California, 1983), p. 59, P. E. Easterling and B. M. W. Knox, *The Cambridge History*

of Classical Literature, Vol. I, *Greek Literature* (Cambridge, 1985), pp. 696, 853f., J. R. Morgan in J. R. Morgan and R. Stoneman, *Greek Fiction: The Greek Novel in Context* (London, 1994), p. 111, n. 10, A. Lesky, *A History of Greek Literature* (London, 1966), pp. 866f. It was also, perhaps, possible to read the (now lost) Greek original of *Apollonius, King of Tyre*, which *might* have been written in the third century AD, though the oldest extant version, in Latin, is of the sixth century, cf. W. S. Teuffel, *A History of Roman Literature* (1873), Vol. II, pp. 559ff., para. 481, B. E. Perry, *The Ancient Romances* (Berkeley and Los Angeles, 1967), pp. 294–324, G. Anderson, *Ancient Fiction* (1984), pp. 6, 52, 105, n. 76, 169f. For Philostratus's connection with pagan religion, see Chapter 12. For the Second Sophistic with which he was linked see M. Grant, *The Antonines* (London, 1994), index s.v. Sophistic, Second.

4 Cf. Hägg, *op. cit.*, pp. 40f., C. Gill and T. P. Wiseman (eds), *Lies and Fiction in the Ancient World* (University of Exeter, 1993), p. 218.

5 Holzberg, *op. cit.* The date of Longus is also discussed by Easterling and Knox, *op. cit.*, p. 895. Perry, *op. cit.*, p. 350, n. 17, suggests the second half of the second century AD. A new edition of Longus's novel has now been published by Aris and Phillips. Meanwhile there is Turner, *op. cit.*

6 Cf. Perry, *Op. cit.*, p. 351.

7 This summary of Longus's plot is adapted from Anderson, *op. cit.*, pp. 137–44.

8 J. R. Morgan in Morgan and Stoneman, *op. cit.*, p. 66.

9 Cf. also above, Paul Turner (n. 2). Lesky, *op. cit.*, p. 868, pronounced that Longus is sometimes lascivious and frivolous.

10 Turner, *op. cit.*, pp. 58f., 77, 81, 121.

11 Hägg, *op. cit.*, p. 96. Hägg, p. 56, also points out that Longus describes the gradual awakening of love, unlike previous novelists who had concentrated more particularly on love at first sight.

12 For Longus's prologue, see Gill and Wiseman, *op. cit.*, p. 218.

13 Cf. Easterling and Knox, *op. cit.*, p. 197.

14 This emphasis on Love (Eros) is derived from an admiration for Nature: Hägg, *op. cit.*, pp. 37f., Easterling and Knox, *op. cit.*, p. 698, E. L. Bowie in K. J. Dover (ed.), *Ancient Greek Literature* (Oxford, 1980), p. 170.

15 Hägg, *op. cit.*, p. 35.

16 P. Levi, *A History of Greek Literature* (Harmondsworth, 1985), p. 452; cf. Lesky, *op. cit.*, p. 867; Turner, *op. cit.*, pp. 15f. In recent times, now that the Greco-Roman novel has come back into fashion, there has been a lot of discussion about the relationship between fact and fiction in ancient writers. For Shakespearian echoes cf. Turner, *op. cit.*, p. 13.

11 ART AND ARCHITECTURE

1 M. Grant, *History of Rome* (London, 1978, 1979), pp. 87f.

2 M. Grant, *The Climax of Rome* (London, 1968, 1993), pp. 91f. For portraits of Septimius Severus cf. H. von Heintze, *Roman Art* (1972, 1990), p. 183, fig. 178, *CAH*, pp. 545, 552f.

3 There are good heads of Julia Domna not only in the Capitoline Museum at Rome but also at Copenhagen, etc.: von Heintze, *op. cit.*, fig. 187. A

sardonyx cameo in the British Museum shows her as Luna (Selene). For the head of another woman of the period at Copenhagen, see J. M. C. Toynbee, *The Art of the Romans* (London, 1965), plate 17; and of a man, G. M. A. Hanfmann, *Roman Art* (New York, 1975), fig. 85.

4 The twist of Caracalla's head may be a deliberate echo of Alexander III the Great, and of Hellenistic monarchs. And the bust may owe something also to the Heracles of Lysippus. There were also colossal sculptures in the Baths of Caracalla, displaying a similar nervous, excitable style. For the religious implications of sculptures on sarcophagi, see next chapter.

5 For example, Capitoline Museum, Rome: R. Delbrueck, *Antike Porträts*, plate 51.

6 For portraits of Severus Alexander, cf. *CAH*, pp. 545, 552f. For the head at Schloss Fasanerie, near Fulda, see von Heintze, *op. cit.*, p. 183, fig. 178. For a statue of him at the National Archaeological Museum in Naples, based on the Doryphorus of Polyclitus, see *ibid.* p. 155, fig. 143 and plate 33. A portrait of an unknown man (*c.* 240) in the Museo Nuovo Capitolino at Rome (discussed by Hanfmann, *op. cit.*, p. 98, cf. fig. 85) shows a similar break with Antonine art.

7 A painted panel (*tondo*) at Berlin (*c.* 199–200), found in Egypt, depicts Septimius and his family, with complete frontality. There are also other Severan wall-paintings at Rome (for example at Villa Manzoni, *c.* 200: see Chapter 12, n. 1) and Ostia and elsewhere in Italy, as well as at Dura-Europus etc.

8 A. W. Lawrence, *Classical Sculpture* (London, 1929), pp. 386f.

9 Dio 75.3.

10 According to one supposition the Baths of Septimius Severus (*Thermae Severianae*) were attached to this building on the Palatine. But they have also, alternatively, been regarded as the precursors of the Baths of Caracalla (on the same site as those Baths). And they have been located across the Tiber as well.

11 The Septizodium was known in the Middle Ages as the Septifolium, or Septemsolis, or Sedes Solis. See now F. Coates, *Classics Chronicle* (winter 1994), p. 13. Did the original building have three, or seven, storeys? (Only three remained at the time of its destruction.)

12 M. Grant, *Art in the Roman Empire* (London, 1995), p. 60.

13 M. Grant, *The Roman Forum* (London, 1970), pp. 169–76. The chariot surmounting the Arch of Septimius was of guilded bronze. For the 'bird's-eye' views, cf. Toynbee, *op. cit.*, pp. 71f. For arches in general, see S. de Maria, *Gli archi onorari di Roma e dell' Italia romana*, Biblioteca Archeologica 7 (Rome, 1988).

14 Toynbee, *op. cit.*, pp. 72f. By way of contrast, on the Palazzo Sacchetti relief, Septimius, receiving a group of togate personages, on a *rostrum*, is shown almost in profile. D. E. Strong, *Roman Imperial Sculpture* (London, 1961), fig. 111.

15 Toynbee, *op. cit.*, pp. 73ff. For Julia Domna, see Chapter 8.

16 M. Grant, *Art in the Roman Empire* (London, 1995), pp. 67–9. The Basilica at Lepcis Magna replaced an earlier building. It was converted into a church in the sixth century AD.

17 For the work of Septimius at Lepcis Magna see J. B. Ward-Perkins, B.

Jones and R. Ling, *The Severan Buildings of Lepcis Magna*, ed. P. M. Kenrick (1994, 1995).

18 For example, the theatre at Sabratha (with fine stage backdrop), JBWP, pp. 377, 381; Baths at Caesarea (Cherchel) (of somewhat uncertain date); temple of the Severan family at Cuicul (Djemila: Chapter 3, n. 1).

19 For example *Propylaea* at Heliopolis (Baalbek): E. Kjellberg and G. Säflund, *Greek and Roman Art* (London, 1968), fig. 147, completed by Philip the Arab (244–9).

20 For example important new Severan building at Ephesus (Selçuk). The central hall of the Serapeum at Pergamum (Bergama) also seems to date from the beginning of the third century.

21 JBWP, pp. 132–4. There are huge fragments in the garden of the Colonna Palace. Caracalla's Temple of Isis was near the Colosseum.

22 Caracalla rebuilt parts of the Circus Maximus at Rome. The House of the Vestals in the Forum, in its present form, is also approximately of this date.

23 Grant, *History of Rome*, chapter 8, p. 112. The egalitarian aspect of the Baths of Caracalla is worth stressing. Hercules, whose figure appears on its capitals, was the patron of the Severan House, as is indicated elsewhere. J. de Laine is now publishing a book on the Baths, which were very expensive. RDJ, p. 16, n. 141.

24 JBWP, pp. 130f.

25 *Ibid.*, pp. 132, 134.

26 Severus Alexander apparently employed some architects (unlike certain imperial sculptors of the same epoch) whose barren classicism betrayed the collapse of artistic ability. A coin shows his Roman Nymphaeum: R. A. G. Carson, *Principal Coins of the Romans*, Vol. II (31 BC–AD 296) (London, 1980), p. 87, no. 747: and another the Colosseum in his reign, J. P. C. Kent and M. and A. Hirmer, *Roman Coins* (London, 1978), plate 119, no. 424. The Aqua Alexandriana dated from AD 226.

27 ROMA AETERNA of Severus Alexander: H. A. Grueber, *Roman Medallions in the British Museum*, p. 40, no. 8.

28 RESTITVTOR VRBIS of Septimius Severus: *BMC*, p. 221 etc.

12 PAGANISM AND CHRISTIANITY

1 Neo-Platonists (encouraged by Ammonius Saccas) and Neo-Pythagoreans were active at this time. For the keen contemporary interest in the after-life, cf. also the Villa Manzoni frescoes (Chapter 11, n. 7) showing the return of Odysseus (Ulysses), which symbolized the soul's return to the land to which it belongs. The Labours of Hercules are depicted, with a similar purpose, on a sarcophagus at the Palazzo Ducale, Mantua: R. Brilliant, *Roman Art* (Oxford, 1974), p. 166, fig. II. 23. The best-known battle sarcophagus is the Ludovisi Sarcophagus, attributed by G. Rodenwaldt, *CAH*, p. 553, to AD 225–30, although it may be later. Cf. also Chapter 11.

2 For texts cf. G. R. S. Mead, *Apollonius of Tyana: The Philosopher-Reformer of the First Century AD*, ed. L. Shephard (New York, 1966), pp. 42ff.

3 *Ibid.*, pp. 55f., cf. pp. 58f. and L. Shephard, *ibid*, p. xxii.

4 Nevertheless, Apollonius of Tyana, a Neo-Pythagorean, represented an (unsuccessful) attempt to set up a sort of rival to Jesus Christ (cf. L. Shephard, in Mead, *op. cit.*, pp. v, xxi. He had long been idolized: for example, he had a cult at Ephesus (Selçuk). Caracalla dedicated a temple to him in 215 (Dio 77.18), and Severus Alexander was said to have kept a statue of him.

5 *SHA, Severus Alexander* 29.2.

6 See also Appendix on the novelistic (fictitious) aspects of Philostratus's work.

7 Mead, *op. cit.*, pp. 28, 155; L. Shephard, *ibid*, pp. v, xxi.

8 Philostratus (if it was he, and not some other member of his family) wrote an open letter to the deceased novelist Chariton.

9 Caracalla visited the tomb of Achilles in 214/15. For Achilles on sarcophagi see D. E. Strong, *Roman Imperial Sculpture* (London, 1961), figs 119, 124.

10 S. Merkle, in J. Tatum (ed.), *The Search for the Ancient Novel* (Baltimore, 1994), pp. 193f. Dictys was a legendary Cretan of Cnossus, a companion of Idomeneus at Troy, and reputed author of a Trojan War diary, actually perhaps composed in the Roman imperial epoch: with 'Dares' it formed the principal source for medieval writers on the Trojan War.

11 For example Jupiter *Praeses Orbis* (*BMC*, pp. 73, 77–94) is the Syrian Baal; cf. Jupiter Heliopolitanus: F. Abbate, *Roman Art* (1972), p. 11, fig. 76, and Jupiter Dolichenus (cf. text). And cf. above, Chapter 1, n. 10.

12 M. Grant, *History of Rome* (London, 1978), pp. 296f. Apollonius of Tyana had burnt incense on the altar of the Sun, and Caracalla may well have derived his entire régime from the Sun-god: cf. *RIC*, p. 82, no. 721. (When he was murdered, he was on his way to do honour to Lunus, the moon (Chapter 4 and n. 3). Geta(?), as the Sun-god (Plate.10), wears a radiant crown, and his right hand is raised in the Sun's magic gesture of benediction (*c.* 200). There were nearly fifty shrines of Mithras in Rome and its suburbs, and eighteen at Ostia, a number of them of Severan date, when Mithraic inscriptions were common. Justin Martyr (*c.* AD 100–65) and Tertullian regarded Mithraism as a diabolical copy of Christianity.

13 They were honoured at the Secular Games (DIS AVSPICIBVS, *BMC*, pp. 29f., 25ff.). There was a naked figure of Hercules on a capital at the baths of Caracalla. Caracalla was devoted to his family patron-god Hercules, and – no doubt for that reason – rejected the identification of Commodus with him. For the Labours of Hercules see above, n. 1, and Chapter 11.

14 And a red jasper from Castlesteads (I. A. Richmond, *Roman Britain* (Harmondsworth, 1955), pp. 196, 211f.) shows Septimius as Serapis. The central hall of the Serapeum (Kizil Avlu) at Pergamum seems to date from the beginning of the third century: JBWP, p. 283, fig. 181.

15 The coins of Elagabalus show the god as CONSERVATOR AVGVSTI (*BMC*, pp. ccxviii, 546, 560f.) and are dedicated SANCT. DEO SOLI ELAGABAL. (Plate 17; *BMC*, pp. 572, 574f.). He became *summus sacerdos* (*BMC*, pp. 565, 585) instead of the traditional 'high priest' (*pontifex maximus*). His celebrations and processions involved public merry-making.

16 Herodian 5.6.6–8 (tr. E. C. Echols); but see also E. M. Smallwood, *The Jews Under Roman Rule*, p. 480, n. 11.

17 M. Grant, *The Climax of Rome* (London, 1968, 1993), pp. 177f.

18 Caracalla's wet-nurse was said to have been a Christian.

19 Orosius 7.17.3, Eusebius, *Chronicon, Severus*, V, Smallwood, *op. cit.*, pp. 488ff.

20 For example Monarchianism, Montanism: cf. text; and Arianism, n. 25 below.

21 For the dispute between Hippolytus and Callistus cf. H. Chadwick, *The Early Church* (Harmondsworth, 1967), pp. 87–9.

22 For example the 'heresies' of Origen; although he was also praised for his significant insistence on orthodoxy. For Numenius cf. Nock, *CAH*, pp. 441, 446, Bidez, *ibid.*, p. 622, Sandbach, *CAH*, XI, p. 700.

23 Another important Christian of the Severan age, according to many, was St Alban. Justin Martyr had died in *c.* AD 165; see n. 12 above.

24 Yet Tertullian never tried to create a theological system. And it has been much debated whether he became a priest of the church at Carthage. But in *c.* 200 he wrote *De Praescriptione Hereticorum* with the intention of ending the controversies between the Church and 'heretics'. Some of his later works, however, produced further controversies, which caused his rupture with the Church.

25 Yet Origen was at pains to link revelation to Greek philosophy. But he was criticized for making the Son inferior to the Father – which earned him condemnation as the precursor of Arianism (the forerunner of Unitarianism).

26 In about the time of Severus Alexander, Marcus Minucius Felix wrote his elegant Latin dialogue the *Octavius*, between pagans and Christians, addressed to the cultivated Roman pagan.

EPILOGUE

1 E. Gibbon, *The Decline and Fall of the Roman Empire*, chapter 5 (end).

APPENDIX: THE LITERARY SOURCES

1 Cf. F. G. Millar, *A Study of Cassius Dio* (Oxford, 1964), *passim.*

2 E. Echols, *Herodian: History of the Roman Empire* (1961), pp. 5ff. It seems that Herodian was born in *c.* 170, possibly at Alexandria.

3 R. Syme also stressed the existence of a (lost) historian of the same period, 'Ignotus', RS/*EB*, p. 48.

4 R. Syme, RS/*EB*, p. 284. Some have seen the emperor Julian the Apostate (361–3) in the work: R. Syme, *Ammianus and the Historia Augusta* (London, 1968), p. 45.

5 For example Galen (lyrical about benefits from Septimius); *The Antonine Itinerary* (probably of Caracallan date); Oppian (read by Caracalla); Sammonicus Serenus (voluminous; he had a library of 62,000 works); Philiscus (cf. Chapter 8); Julius Africanus (who dedicated his encyclopaedia to Severus Alexander); Celsus; Minucius Felix (see Chapter 12, n. 26).

6 For example Aurelius Victor (cf. H. W. Bird (ed.) *Aurelius Victor: Liber de Caesaribus* (Liverpool, 1994).

7 See Further Reading. On the Syrian 'atelier' monetary system at Antioch, cf. K. Butcher, *Numismatic Chronicle* (1988), pp. 63ff, *JRS* 84 (1994), p. 257.

FURTHER READING

Amedick, A. *Die Sarkophage und Darstellungen aus dem Menschenleben*, Berlin, 1991

Anderson, G. *Philostratus*, London, 1986

Andreae, E. W. *Hatra*, 2 vols, Leipzig, 1908, 1912

Bainton, R. *The Penguin History of Christianity*, 2 vols, Harmondsworth, 1964, 1967

Balsdon, J. P. V. D. *Roman Women*, London, 1962

Barbieri, G. *L'albo senatorio da Settimio Severo a Carino*, Rome, 1952

Barnes, T. D. *The Sources of the Historia Augusta*, Brussels, 1978

Basset, H. J. *Macrinus and Diadumenianus*, Ann Arbor, 1920

Baynes, N. H. *The Historia Augusta: Its Date and Purpose*, Oxford, 1926

Benko, S. J. and O'Rourke, J. J. *The Catacombs and the Colosseum: The Roman Empire in the Setting of Primitive Christianity*, Valley Forge, 1971

Bertrand, E. *Philostrate et son école*, Paris, 1886

Bihlmeyer, K. *Die Syrischen Kaiser zu Rom (211–235) und das Christentum*, Rottenburg, 1916

Bird, H. W. (ed.) *Aurelius Victor: Liber de Caesaribus*, Liverpool, 1994.

Birley, A. *Septimius Severus: The African Emperor*, London, 1971

Boer, H. G. W. *De Julia Mamaea Severi Alexandri Matre*, Utrecht, 1911

Bowersock, G. W. *Greek Sophists in the Roman Empire*, 1969

Bowersock, G. W. *et al.*, *Edward Gibbon and the Decline and Fall of the Roman Empire*, Cambridge, Mass., 1977

Brilliant, R. *The Arch of Septimius Severus in the Roman Forum*, Memoirs of the American Academy in Rome, no. 29, 1967

Buck, P. C. and Mattingly, D. J. (eds) *Roman Tripolitania*, Oxford, 1994

Butler, O. F. *Studies in the Life of Elagabalus*, Ann Arbor, 1910

Cadiou, R. *Introduction au système d'Origène*, Paris, 1932

Campbell, J. B. *The Emperor and his Army*, Oxford, 1964

Canfield, L. H. *The Early Persecutions of the Christians*, New York, 1913

Carson, R. A. G. *Principal Coins of the Romans*, Vol. II (31 BC–AD 296), London, 1980

Ceulenaar, A. de *Essai sur la vie et règne de Septime Sévère*, Brussels, 1874, 1970

Chadwick, H. *The Early Church*, Harmondsworth, 1967

Colledge, M. A. R. *The Parthians*, London, 1967

Colomba, G. M. *Settimio Severo e gli imperatori africani*, Milan, 1935

Cook, S. A. *et al.* (eds) *Cambridge Ancient History*, Vol. XII (*The Roman Crisis and Recovery* AD *193–324*), Cambridge, 1939

Crook, J. *Consilium Principis*, Cambridge, 1953

Cumont, F. *Afterlife in Roman Paganism*, New Haven, 1922

Davies, J. G. *The Early Christian Church*, London, 1965

Dodds, E. R. *Pagan and Christian in an Age of Anxiety*, Cambridge, 1965

Dorey, T. A. (ed.) *Latin Biography*, London, 1967

Downey, G. *A History of Antioch in Syria from Seleucus to the Arab Conquest*, Princeton, 1961

Duncan Jones, R. *Money and Government in the Roman Empire*, Cambridge, 1994

Durry, M. *Les cohortes prétoriennes*, Paris, 1938

Dzielska, M. *Apollonius of Tyana in Legend and History*, Probleme e Ricerche di Storia Antica 10, Rome, 1986

Felletti Maj, B. M. *Iconografia imperiale*, Vol. II, *Da Severo a Marco Aurelio Carino*, Rome, 1958

Forquet de Dorne, C. *Les Césars africains et syriens et l'anarchie militaire*, Studia Historica 72, Rome, 1905, 1976

Frend, W. H. C. *The Early Church: From the Beginnings to 461*, London, 1982 (1965)

Fuchs, R. *Geschichte des Kaisers Lucius Septimius Severus*, Vienna, 1884

Garnsey, M. P. and Saller, R. *The Roman Empire: Economy, Society and Culture*, Berkeley and Los Angeles, 1987

Gibbon, E. *The Decline and Fall of the Roman Empire*, London, 1776–88 (Penguin and Everyman edns, 1994)

Grant, M. *The Army of the Caesars*, London, 1974

Grant, M. *The Climax of Rome*, London, 1968, 1993

Grant, M. *Greeks and Romans: A Social History*, London, 1992

Grant, M. *History of Rome*, London, 1978, 1979

Grant, M. *The Roman Emperors*, London, 1985

Grant, R. M. *Early Christianity and Society: Seven Studies*, New York, 1977

Halsberghe, G. *Sol Invictus*, Leiden, 1972

Hammond, M. *The Antonine Monarchy*, Memoirs of the American Academy at Rome, no. 19, 1959

Hartke, W. *Römische Kinderkaiser*, Berlin, 1951

Hasebroek, J. *Untersuchungen zur Geschichte des Kaisers Septimius Severus*, Heidelberg, 1921

Hay, J. S. *The Amazing Emperor Heliogabalus*, London, 1911

Haynes, D. E. L. and Hirst, P. E. D. *Arcus Argentariorum*, London, 1939

Historia-Augusta-Colloquium, Bonn, 1964/5

Honoré, T. *Emperors and Lawyers*, London, 1981

Honoré, T. *Ulpian*, Oxford, 1956

Hopkins, R. V. M. *The Life of Alexander Severus*, Cambridge, 1907

Howe, L. L. *The Praetorian Prefect from Commodus to Diocletian*, Chicago, 1942

Jardé, A. *Etudes critiques sur la vie at la règne de Sévère Alexandre*, Paris, 1925

Joneste, P. F. B. *The Twelve Labours of Hercules on Roman Sarcophagi*, Rome, 1992

Kent, J. P. C. and Hirmer, M. and A. *Roman Coins*, London, 1978

Keyes, C. W. *The Rise of the Equites in the Third Century of the Roman Empire*, Princeton, 1915

Kolbe, F. *Literarische Beziehungen zwischen Cassius Dio, Herodian und der Historia Augusta*, Bonn, 1972

Kunkel, W. *An Introduction to Roman Legal and Constitutional History*, Oxford, 1966

La Faye, E. de *Origen and his Work*, London, 1926

Lambrechts, P. *La composition du sénat romain de Septime Sévère*, Budapest, 1937

Lane Fox, R. *Pagans and Christians*, London, 1986

Lortz, J. *Tertullian als Apologet*, 2 vols, Münster, 1927/8

McCann, A. M. *The Portraits of Septimius Severus*, Memoirs of the American Academy at Rome, no. 30, 1968

Macmullen, R. *Christianizing the Roman Empire (AD 100–400)*, New Haven, 1984

Macmullen, R. *Paganism in the Roman Empire*, New Haven, 1981

Markus, R. A. *Christianity in the Roman World*, London, 1974

Mattingly, D. J. *Tripolitania*, London, 1995

Mattingly, H. *Coins of the Roman Empire in the British Museum*, Vol. V (Pertinax to Elagabalus), London, 1950

Mattingly, H. *Roman Coins*, London, 1928, 1960, 1962

Mattingly, H. and Sydenham, E. A. *Roman Imperial Coinage*, Vol. IV, Part 1, London, 1936

Mead, G. R. S. *Apollonius of Tyana: The Philosopher-Reformer of the First Century AD*, ed. L. Shephard, New Hyde Park, N.Y. 1966

Millar, F. G. *The Roman Near East*, Cambridge, Mass., 1993

Millar, F. G. *A Study of Cassius Dio*, Oxford, 1964

Momigliano, A. *On Pagans, Jews and Christians*, Middletown, Conn., 1957

Momigliano, A. (ed.), *The Conflict between Paganism and Christianity*, Oxford, 1963

Murphy, G. J. *The Reign of the Emperor Lucius Septimius Severus from the Evidence of the Inscriptions*, Philadelphia, 1945

Nicholas, B. *An Introduction to Roman Law*, Oxford, 1962

Oliva, P. *Pannonia and the Onset of Crisis in the Roman Empire*, Prague, 1962

Parker, H. M. D. *The Roman Legions*, Cambridge, 1971

Passerini, A. *Le coorte pretorie*, Rome, 1939

Perowne, S. *The Caesars' Wives*, London, 1974

Peterson, E. Eισ θεοσ: *Epigraphische Formgeschichtliche und Religionsgeschichtliche untersuchungen*, Göttingen, 1926

Platnauer, M. *The Life and Reign of the Emperor Lucius Septimius Severus*, Oxford, 1918, 1965

Plew, J. *Marius Maximus als direkte und indirekte Quelle der Scriptores Historiae Augustae*, Strasburg, 1878

Puliatti, S. *Il De Jure Fisci di Callistrato e il processo fiscale in età severiana*, Milan, 1994

Ragette, F. *Baalbek*, London, 1980

Raven, S. *Rome in Africa*, London, 1969, 1993

Reusch, W. *Der Historische Wert der Caracalla-Vita in den Scriptores Historiae Augustae*, Klio Beiheft 24, 1931

Reville, J. *La réligion à Rome sous les Sévères*, Paris, 1886

Richmond, I. A. *Roman Britain*, Harmondsworth, 1955, 1963

Roman Empresses, The Vol. II, London, 1899

Rostovtzeff, M. *Social and Economic History of the Roman Empire*, 2nd edn, ed. P. M. Fraser, Oxford, 1957

Schulz, F. *Principles of Roman Law*, Oxford, 1936, 1956

Schulz, O. T. A. *Der römische Kaiser Caracalla: Genie, Wahnsinn oder Verbrechen*, Leipzig, 1909

Schulz, O. T. A. *Vom Prinzipat zum Dominat*, Paderborn, 1919

Sherwin-White, A. N. *The Roman Citizenship*, Oxford, 1939, 1973

Stein, A. *Der römische Ritterstand*, Munich, 1927

Stern, H. *Date et destinataire de l'Histoire Auguste*, Paris, 1953

Stoneman, R. *Palmyra and its Empire*, Ann Arbor, 1992

Straub, J. *Heidnische Geschichte: Apologetik in der christlichen Spätantike: Untersuchungen über Zeit und Tendenz der Historia Augusta*, Bonn, 1963

Sutherland, C. H. V. *Roman Coins*, London, 1974

Syme, R. *Ammianus and the Historia Augusta*, London, 1968

Syme, R. *Emperors and Biography*, Oxford, 1971

Syme, R. *The Historia Augusta: A Call for Clarity*, Bonn, 1971

Temporini, H. and Haase, W. (eds) *Aufstieg und Niedergang der römischen Welt*, Berlin and New York, many vols.

Thiele, W. *De Severo Alexandro Imperatore*, Berlin, 1909

Thompson, J. S. *Aufstände und Protestaktionen in Imperium Romanum*, Bonn, 1990

Toynbee, J. M. C. *Roman Medallions*, New York, 1944 (rev. edn, W. E. Metcalf, New York, 1986)

Turcan, R. *Historia Augusta: Vies de Macrin, Diaduménien, Héliogabale*, Paris, 1993

Turner, P. (ed.) *Longus: Daphnis and Chloe*, Harmondsworth, 1968

Turton, G. *The Syrian Princesses: The Women who Ruled Rome AD 193–235*, London, 1974

Vergara Caffarelli, E., Caputo, G. and Bianchi Bandinelli, K. *The Buried City: Excavations at Lepcis Magna*, Rome, 1963

Wacher, J. (ed.) *The Roman World*, 2 vols, London, 1987

Walser, G. and Pekáry, T. *Die Krisis des römischen Reiches*, Berlin, 1962

Ward-Perkins, J. B. *Roman Imperial Architecture*, Harmondsworth, 1981

Ward-Perkins, J. B. *The Severan Buildings of Lepcis Magna*, ed. P. M. Kenrick, London, 1994/5

Watson, G. R. *The Roman Soldier*, London, 1969

Webster, G. *The Roman Imperial Army of the First Two Centuries AD*, London, 1969, 1985

Weinreich, O. *Neue Urkunden zur Serapis-Religion*, Tübingen, 1919

Westermann, W. L. and Schiller, A. A. *Apokrimata: Decisions of Septimius Severus on Legal Matters*, New York, 1954

Wheeler, R. E. M. *Rome Beyond the Imperial Frontiers*, London, 1954

Widmer, W. *Kaisertum, Rom und Welt in Herodian*, Zurich, 1967

Wirth, A. *Quaestiones Severianae*, Leipzig, 1888

INDEX

Abgar VIII (IX) 97
Abraham 75
Achaea, Achaia (Greece) 75, 83
Achilles 64, 104
Achilles Tatius 54, 58
Adiabene 97
aediles, curule 51
Aemilianus, Asellius *see* Asellius
Aequitas 43, 99
Aesculapius (Asclepius) 19
Aethiopica 33, 100
Africa, *Africitas* 1ff., 5, 8, 11, 28, 49,
    53, 65, 68ff., 72, 78, 80, 82,
    93, 97
Africanus, Julius 105
Agricola, Cnaeus Julius 30
Agrippina the younger 45
Alamanni 32, 86; *see also* Germany,
    Germans
Alban, St 110
Albanum (Albano) 15, 35, 97
Albinus, Clodius 7, 10f., 18, 29,
    45, 94
Alexander III the Great 19, 26, 31f.,
    49, 62
Alexander, Severus *see* Severus
    Alexander
Alexandria 31, 81ff., 95, 105
Alexianus *see* Severus Alexander
Altar of Peace (Ara Pacis, Rome) 60
Ammianus Marcellinus 105
Ammonius Saccas 83, 103
Annia Faustina 25
Annona 40, 99

Antioch 8f., 23f., 47, 94, 97, 106
antoninianus see coinage
Antoninus Pius 30
Apamea (Qalaat al-Mudik) 100
Aphrodisias (Geyre) 60, 63
Apollonius of Tyana 5, 74ff., 79,
    100, 103f.
Apollonius of Tyre 101
Apollonius Rhodius 54
Apronianus, Cassius *see* Cassius
    Apronianus
Aqua Alexandriana 103
Aquilia Severa 25
Aquincum (Budapest) 97
Arabic 100
Ara Pacis *see* Altar of Peace
Arca Caesarea ad Libanum (Arqa)
    26, 47f.
Arch of the Bankers (*argentarii*) 46,
    60, 67f., 70, 105
Arch of Macrinus (Diana
    Veteranorum) 72
Arch of Septimius Severus 5, 60, 66,
    69, 102
Arch of Septimius Severus (Lepcis
    Magna) 46, 60f., 68f., 95
Arch of Titus 60, 66
Arch of Trajan (Beneventum) 67
Arcus Argentariorum *see* Arch of
    the Bankers
Ardashir (Artaxerxes) I 32, 97
argentarii see Arch of the Bankers
Arianism 105
Aristides of Miletus 54

Artabanus V 31f.
Artaxerxes *see* Ardashir
Artemis *see* Diana
Asclepius *see* Aesculapius
Asellius Aemilianus 9
Asia 69, 71
Asia Minor 9, 54, 63, 65, 70, 81f.
asses see coinage
Assyria 66
Athens 47, 63, 81
Augustus 10, 13, 26f., 36f., 60, 86
aurei see coinage
Aurelius, Marcus 1ff., 11, 18, 20, 49, 60f., 67, 78
Aurelius, Victor *see* Victor
aurum coronarium 42
Auspex, Pollienus *see* Pollienus
Avidius Cassius 11
Avitus, Julius 24, 47
Avitus Bassianus, Varius *see* Elagabalus

Baal 45, 72, 79
Baalbek *see* Heliopolis
Bacchus (Dionysus) 69f., 77f.
Barsemius 10
Bassianus, Julius 45
Baths of Caracalla 5, 71f.
Baths of Nero 73
Baths of Trajan 72
Baths, Vaulted Hunting (Lepcis Magna) 70
Beneventum (Benevento) 67
Berbers 7f.
Berytus (Beirut) 95
Bithynia 2, 11
boarii, negotiantes 67
Boddhisatva 61
Bodotria (Firth of Forth) 12, 98
bonuses *see* finance
Bosphorus *see* Byzantium
Britain, Britannia 1, 7f., 10f., 15, 19f., 30, 38f., 42, 96, 98
Buddhists 61
Bulla Felix 17
Byzantine Empire 61
Byzantium (Constantinople, Istanbul) 9f., 80

Caesarea, Arca, ad Libanum *see* Arca
Caesarea (Iol, Cherchel) 22, 103
Caesarea Maritima 83
Caledonia 8
Callistus 81, 83, 105
Campania 96
Caracalla 3ff., 8, 11, 18f., 18–24, 26, 30ff., 36ff., 40, 42f., 46f., 49f., 62, 66, 68f., 71f., 76, 78, 83, 95f., 99f., 102–5
Carnuntum (Petronell) 7, 97
Carpow 30
Carrhae (Altibaşak) 22
Carthage, Carthaginians, Punic 7, 82, 97, 105
Cassius Apronianus 87
Castlesteads 96
Celsus 83, 105
Celtic 29
Ceres (Demeter) 48
Cervidius Scaevola, Quintus 49f.
Chariton 54, 104
Chester *see* Deva
Chloe 54–8, 100
Christians, Christianity 5
Cilicia 87
Cilician Gates (Külek Boğazi) 9
Cirta (Constantine) 45, 93
Cissia 75
Clement of Alexandria 81
Clodius Albinus *see* Albinus
Cnossus 104
Coele 98
coinage 93–6, 98ff., 106
collegia 41
Colosseum 73, 78, 103
Column of Aurelius 60f.
Column of Trajan 67
Comazon Eutychianus 27, 95
Commagene 78
Commodus 1f., 9, 18, 36, 39, 64, 78, 87, 95, 104
Concordia 36
consilium see Council
Constantine I the Great 89
Constantinople *see* Byzantium
Constitutio Antoniniana 30f., 42, 46f., 52, 98
constitutiones 49

coronarium, aurum see aurum
   coronarium
Council, imperial, senatorial 16, 27,
   31, 37, 48, 51, 85
Crete 76, 104
Ctesiphon (Taysafun) 8, 29, 95
Cuicul (Djemila) 95, 97, 103
curule aediles *see* aediles
Cybele 78
Cynics 75
Cyzicus (Balkiz) 9

Dacia 1, 9, 11
Dalmatia 2, 87
Damis 75
Damophyle 75
Danube (Ister), River 8, 15, 28, 31,
   36, 38, 86, 93
Daphnis 54–8, 100
Dares 104
Darius I 75
Decius, Trajanus *see* Trajanus Decius
dediticii 31
Demeter *see* Ceres
Demetrius 83
Demosthenes 88
denarii see coinage
Deva (Chester) 98
Diadumenian 23f., 95f.
Diana Veteranorum (Zama) 72
Dictys 76, 104
Didius Julianus 2, 7f., 15, 39, 94f.
Dio Cassius 10f., 21, 23, 27, 36,
   41f., 64, 86f., 105
Dio Chrysostom 75, 87
Diocletian 89
Dionysophanes 56
Dionysus *see* Bacchus
Doliche (Tell Duluk) 78
Domna, Julia *see* Julia Domna
Dorcon 35
Doryphorus 102
dupondii see coinage
Dura-Europus 29, 61, 69, 80f., 97,
   102
dysentery *see* health

Eburacum (York) 8, 30, 98
Edessa (Urfa) 97; *see also* Osrhoene

edicta, rescripts 95, 100
Egypt 29, 71, 74, 76, 78, 83, 97, 99
Elagabalus 15, 24f., 27f., 36f., 43,
   47f., 50f., 62, 72f., 78ff., 85,
   99f., 104
Emesa (Homs) 24, 45, 49, 54, 72,
   78f., 100
Ephesus (Selçuk) 78, 99, 103f.
equites see knights
Eretria 75
Eros (Love) 55–8, 101
Euphrates, River 9, 31
Euripides 54
Eusebius 83

Faustina, Annia *see* Annia Faustina
Faustina the younger 95
Fecunditas 96
Felicitas 100
Felix, Minucius *see* Minucius Felix
finance, taxation, inflation 1f., 23,
   31ff., 35, 38–44, 86, 99
Flavian Palace 65
Fronto, Marcus Cornelius 94
Fulda 96, 102
Fulvia Pia 7, 95
Fulvius Plautianus *see* Plautianus

Galen 100, 105
Gallia Belgica 2
Gallia Lugdunensis 7; *see also*
   Lugdunum
Games 41, 76
Gannys 24f., 47
Garamantes 29; *see also* Germany
Gaul 81, 99; *see also* Gallia Belgica,
   Lugdunensis
genus humanum, common homeland
   29, 31
Germany, Germans 1, 12, 27, 30,
   43, 48
Germany, Lower 2, 11
Germany, Upper, 11
Geta 3, 11, 19f., 21ff., 26, 30f., 37,
   42, 46, 50, 62, 66f., 95f., 104
Geta, Lucius Septimius 16
Geta, Publius Septimius 93, 95
Gnostics 81
Golas 29

guard, praetorian, bodyguards 2, 14f., 37, 44, 48, 51, 94f., 98
guilds see collegia

Hadrian 30, 63, 72
Hadrumetum (Sousse) 11
Hatra (Al-Hadr) 8, 10, 29, 46, 61, 69
health, illness 3f., 19, 32, 47, 95f.
Hebrew see Jews
Heliodorus 53f., 100
Heliogabalus see Elagabalus
Heliopolis (Baalbek) 103f.
Helvius Successus see Successus
Hera see Juno
Heracles, Hercules 64, 69f., 77f., 97, 102ff.
Herodian 94, 96, 105
Herodotus 54
Heroicus 76
Hippolytus 48, 81, 105
Hispania Tarraconensis 12
Homer (Iliad, Odyssey) 54, 76
honestiores 31, 49, 52
horoscopes 13, 45
humiliores 31, 49, 52

Iamblichus 54
Idomeneus 104
'Ignotus' 105
Ilium see Troy
illness see health
Illyrians 15
India 61, 75, 99
Indulgentia 96f.
Ionia 75
Iran see Persia
Irenaeus 81f.
Isa Silurum (Caerleon) 98
Isis 78, 103
Issus (Deli Çay) 9
Ister, River see Danube
Italy, Italians 1, 8f., 17, 31, 35, 63, 70, 102

Janus 96
Jesus Christ see Christians, Christianity
Jews, Hebrews 80, 84

Judaea (Palestine) 83
Judah I the Prince 80
Julia Domna 4, 16, 18, 21f., 24, 28f., 45, 64, 68, 70, 74, 76f., 79, 84, 100ff.
Julia Maesa 24f., 27, 45, 47, 79
Julia Mamaea 5, 15, 26f., 37f., 44f., 47f., 75, 81, 84, 100
Julia Paula 25
Julia Soaemias 24ff., 45, 47, 100
Julian the Apostate 26, 105
Julianus, Didius see Didius Julianus
Julius Africanus see Africanus, Julius
Julius Avitus see Avitus, Julius
Julius Bassianus see Bassianus, Julius
Juno (Hera), Juno Moneta 7, 43
Jupiter (Zeus) 73f., 104
Justin Martyr 104f.

kind, taxation in see finance
knights (equites) 1, 11, 41

Laetitia 99
Lambaesis (Tazzoult) 97
Laodicea (Latakia) 97
Leonides 83
Lepcis Magna 7, 46, 60f., 77, 95, 102
Lesbos 55f.
Liberalitas 41, 96
Longi, Pompeii 55
Longus 5, 54–8, 76, 81, 84, 90, 100f.
Love see Eros
Lower Moesia see Moesia
Lower Pannonia see Pannonia
Ludovisi Sarcophagus 64, 103
Lugdunum (Lyon) 81, 94
Luna (Selene) 102
Lunus 22, 96, 104
Lycaenion 56, 58
Lycaonia 63
Lydia 29
Lysippus 102

Macrinus 22ff., 32, 36f., 43, 47, 49, 96, 99
Macrinus, Seius (?) Sallustius 48
Maecenas 27, 36

Maesa, Julia *see* Julia Maesa
Mamaea, Julia *see* Julia Mamaea
Marcellus, Sextus Varius *see* Varius
Marciana, Paccia *see* Paccia
   Marciana
Marcus Aurelius *see* Aurelius
Marius, Gaius 13
Marius Marcellus, Sextus 24
Marius Maximus 89f.
Mars 67
Masurius Sabinus 50f.
Mauretania Caesariensis 22, 29
Maximinus I Thrax 15, 27
Maximus, Marius *see* Marius
Mediolanum (Milan) 2
Melkart *see* Heracles
Menander 54
Mesopotamia 8, 29, 32, 61, 66f., 86
Messalina 45
Methymna 56
Miletus (Balat) 54
Minucius Felix, Marcus 105
Mithras 77f., 86, 104
Moesia 1, 93
Moguntiacum (Mainz) 2
Monarchianism 105
Moneta *see* finance, Juno
monotheism 5, 74, 77
Montanists 81ff., 105
Moon *see* Selene
Mytilene 55

negotiantes boarii see boarii
Neo-Platonists 77, 83, 103
Neo-Pythagoreans *see* Pythagoras
Nero 73
Nicaea (Iznik) 9, 87, 94
Niger, Pescennius *see* Pescennius
   Niger
Nike *see* Victory
Novius Rufus, Lucius 12
Numenius 105
numeri 31, 34, 36, 97
nymphaea 65, 73, 103

Octavius 115
Odysseus (Ulysses), *Odyssey* 54, 103
Oppian 105
Orbiana 26, 48

Origen 48, 81, 83f., 105
Orpheus 75
Osrhoene 1, 8, 34, 97; *see also*
   Edessa
Ostia 102, 104

Paccia Marciana 45, 96
Palestine *see* Judaea
Palmyra (Tadmor) 29, 34, 61, 69
Pan 56
Pannonia 1f., 7, 9, 28
Pantaenus 81
Papinian 16, 49f., 52, 100
Parthenius 54
Parthia, Parthians 4, 8, 10, 18, 22ff.,
   29–32, 39, 41f., 46, 49, 60f., 66,
   69, 86, 97ff.
Paula, Julia *see* Julia Paula
Paulus, Julius 50ff.
pay *see* finance
Peace, Altar of *see* Altar of Peace
Pentelic marble 66
Perga (Murtana) 75
Pergamum (Bergama) 103f.
Perinthus (Marmaraereğlisi, Ereğli)
   9
Perpetua 80
Perpetuitas 26
Persia, Persians 4, 29, 32, 61, 86
Pertinax 1f., 7, 9, 93ff., 99
Pertinax (son) 93f.
Pescennius Niger 2, 7, 9, 11f., 14,
   29, 45, 76f., 80, 94
Philetas 56, 58
Philiscus 47, 104
philosophers 62, 64, 74f., 100
Philostratus 47, 53, 74ff., 79, 101,
   104
Phoenicia, Phoenice 26, 51, 76
Phraotes 75
Plato, Platonists 103
Plautianus 3, 14ff., 22, 41, 46, 67,
   95
Plautilla 16, 67
Poimenika 57
Pollienus Auspex 93
Polyclitus 102
Pompeii Longi 55
pontifex maximus 96, 104

Pontus 2, 11
praetorian guard *see* guard
Protesilaus 76
Providentia 94
Prusa ad Hypium (Brusa) 75, 87
Pudicitia 47, 83
Punic *see* Carthage
Pythagoras, Pythagoreans, Neo-Pythagoreans 72, 103f.

Raetia 1
reliefs 60f.
Restitutor Monetae see coinage
Restitutor Urbis 73, 103
Rhaetia *see* Raetia
Rhenus (Rhine), River 8, 15, 32, 86, 93
Rufus, Lucius Novius *see* Novius

Sabinian School 50
Saccas, Ammonius *see* Ammonius
Sallustius Marcrinus, Seius (?) *see* Macrinus
Sammonicus Serenus 105
Sappho 75
Sarapis *see* Serapis
sarcophagi 63f., 76, 102f.
Sarmatians 9
Savaria (Szombathely) 7
Scaevola, Quintus Cervidius *see* Cervidius
Scapula 82
Scotland *see* Caledonia
Sejanus, Lucius Aelius 16
Selene 96
Septimius Geta, Lucius *see* Geta
Septimius Geta, Publius *see* Geta
Septizonium, Septizodium 65, 102
Serapis (Sarapis) 61, 70, 78, 96, 103f.
Serenus, Sammonicus *see* Sammonicus
sestertii see coinage
Severa, Aquilia *see* Aquilia Severa
Severus Alexander 15, 24–8, 36f., 43, 47–51, 62, 72f., 75, 80, 85, 96, 99, 102–5

Sicily 7
Sidamar(i)a (Ambar Arasi) 63
Silver-Workers, Arch of the *see* Arch of the Bankers
slaves 37
Socrates 53
Sol (Sun) 29, 65, 77ff., 104
Sophists 53, 74ff., 104
Spain *see* Hispania (Tarraconensis)
Stoics 75, 82
Strymon (Struma), River 32
subsidies *see* finance
Successus, Helvius (father of Pertinax) 1
Suheina 100
Sulla, Lucius Cornelius 13
Sulpicianus 2
Sun *see* Sol
superstition 13, 45, 65, 74
syncretism 74
Syria 1ff., 9, 24, 26–30, 45ff., 49, 61, 70, 74, 77, 79, 96ff., 106; *see also* Phoenicia (Phoenice)

Tacitus 45
Taurus (Toros), Mts 9
Tava (Tay), River 30
taxation *see* finance
Tertullian 5, 81ff., 104f.
Theocritus 57
Thessaly 47
Thrace 76, 97
Tiber, River 67
Tiberius 16
Tigris, River 29
Tinurtium (Tournus) 12
Titus 60
Trajan 28, 34, 67
Trajanus Decius 83
Tripolitana 7, 28
Troy, Trojan war 76, 104f.
Tyana (near Kemerhisar) 74ff., 79, 100, 103f.
Tyre (Es-Sur) 51, 83, 97, 101

Ulpian 15, 17, 48, 50ff.
Ulysses *see* Odysseus
Unitarianism 105

Varius Marcellus, Sextus 100
Verus, Lucius 2, 20, 61
Vespasian 7
Vesta, Vestals 96
Via Appia 65
Via Flaminia 22
Victor, Aurelius 106
Victor (bishop) 81
Victory 48, 67

Vologases V 9, 97

Xenophon of Ephesus
  53f.
Xenophon (historian) 54

York *see* Eburacum

Zeus *see* Jupiter

Michael Grant is one of the world's
greatest writers on ancient history. He was
formerly a Fellow of Trinity College,
Cambridge, Professor of Humanities at
the University of Edinburgh and Vice-
Chancellor of the University of Khartoum
and the Queen's University of Belfast. He
has published over fifty books.